# Thoughts o

# Present Disc......

## And Speeches

Edmund Burke

(Editor: Henry Morley)

**Alpha Editions**

This edition published in 2023

ISBN : 9789357943086

Design and Setting By
**Alpha Editions**
www.alphaedis.com
Email - info@alphaedis.com

# Contents

# INTRODUCTION

Edmund Burke was born at Dublin on the first of January, 1730. His father was an attorney, who had fifteen children, of whom all but four died in their youth. Edmund, the second son, being of delicate health in his childhood, was taught at home and at his grandfather's house in the country before he was sent with his two brothers Garrett and Richard to a school at Ballitore, under Abraham Shackleton, a member of the Society of Friends. For nearly forty years afterwards Burke paid an annual visit to Ballitore.

In 1744, after leaving school, Burke entered Trinity College, Dublin. He graduated B.A. in 1748; M.A., 1751. In 1750 he came to London, to the Middle Temple. In 1756 Burke became known as a writer, by two pieces. One was a pamphlet called "A Vindication of Natural Society." This was an ironical piece, reducing to absurdity those theories of the excellence of uncivilised humanity which were gathering strength in France, and had been favoured in the philosophical works of Bolingbroke, then lately published. Burke's other work published in 1756, was his "Essay on the Sublime and Beautiful."

At this time Burke's health broke down. He was cared for in the house of a kindly physician, Dr. Nugent, and the result was that in the spring of 1757 he married Dr. Nugent's daughter. In the following year Burke made Samuel Johnson's acquaintance, and acquaintance ripened fast into close friendship. In 1758, also, a son was born; and, as a way of adding to his income, Burke suggested the plan of "The Annual Register."

In 1761 Burke became private secretary to William Gerard Hamilton, who was then appointed Chief Secretary to Ireland. In April, 1763, Burke's services were recognised by a pension of £300 a year; but he threw this up in April, 1765, when he found that his services were considered to have been not only recognised, but also bought. On the 10th of July in that year (1765) Lord Rockingham became Premier, and a week later Burke, through the good offices of an admiring friend who had come to know him in the newly-founded Turk's Head Club, became Rockingham's private secretary. He was now the mainstay, if not the inspirer, of Rockingham's policy of pacific compromise in the vexed questions between England and the American colonies. Burke's elder brother, who had lately succeeded to his father's property, died also in 1765, and Burke sold the estate in Cork for £4,000.

Having become private secretary to Lord Rockingham, Burke entered Parliament as member for Wendover, and promptly took his place among the leading speakers in the House.

On the 30th of July, 1766, the Rockingham Ministry went out, and Burke wrote a defence of its policy in "A Short Account of a late Short Administration." In 1768 Burke bought for £23,000 an estate called Gregories or Butler's Court, about a mile from Beaconsfield. He called it by the more territorial name of Beaconsfield, and made it his home. Burke's endeavours to stay the policy that was driving the American colonies to revolution, caused the State of New York, in 1771, to nominate him as its agent. About May, 1769, Edmund Burke began the pamphlet here given, *Thoughts on the Present Discontents.* It was published in 1770, and four editions of it were issued before the end of the year. It was directed chiefly against Court influence, that had first been used successfully against the Rockingham Ministry. Allegiance to Rockingham caused Burke to write the pamphlet, but he based his argument upon essentials of his own faith as a statesman. It was the beginning of the larger utterance of his political mind.

Court influence was strengthened in those days by the large number of newly-rich men, who bought their way into the House of Commons for personal reasons and could easily be attached to the King's party. In a population of 8,000,000 there were then but 160,000 electors, mostly nominal. The great land-owners generally held the counties. When two great houses disputed the county of York, the election lasted fourteen days, and the costs, chiefly in bribery, were said to have reached three hundred thousand pounds. Many seats in Parliament were regarded as hereditary possessions, which could be let at rental, or to which the nominations could be sold. Town corporations often let, to the highest bidders, seats in Parliament, for the benefit of the town funds. The election of John Wilkes for Middlesex, in 1768, was taken as a triumph of the people. The King and his ministers then brought the House of Commons into conflict with the freeholders of Westminster. Discontent became active and general. "Junius" began, in his letters, to attack boldly the King's friends, and into the midst of the discontent was thrown a message from the Crown asking for half a million, to make good a shortcoming in the Civil List. Men asked in vain what had been done with the lost money. Confusion at home was increased by the great conflict with the American colonies; discontents, ever present, were colonial as well as home. In such a time Burke endeavoured to show by what pilotage he would have men weather the storm.

H. M.

# THOUGHTS ON THE PRESENT DISCONTENTS

It is an undertaking of some degree of delicacy to examine into the cause of public disorders. If a man happens not to succeed in such an inquiry, he will be thought weak and visionary; if he touches the true grievance, there is a danger that he may come near to persons of weight and consequence, who will rather be exasperated at the discovery of their errors than thankful for the occasion of correcting them. If he should be obliged to blame the favourites of the people, he will be considered as the tool of power; if he censures those in power, he will be looked on as an instrument of faction. But in all exertions of duty something is to be hazarded. In cases of tumult and disorder, our law has invested every man, in some sort, with the authority of a magistrate. When the affairs of the nation are distracted, private people are, by the spirit of that law, justified in stepping a little out of their ordinary sphere. They enjoy a privilege of somewhat more dignity and effect than that of idle lamentation over the calamities of their country. They may look into them narrowly; they may reason upon them liberally; and if they should be so fortunate as to discover the true source of the mischief, and to suggest any probable method of removing it, though they may displease the rulers for the day, they are certainly of service to the cause of Government. Government is deeply interested in everything which, even through the medium of some temporary uneasiness, may tend finally to compose the minds of the subjects, and to conciliate their affections. I have nothing to do here with the abstract value of the voice of the people. But as long as reputation, the most precious possession of every individual, and as long as opinion, the great support of the State, depend entirely upon that voice, it can never be considered as a thing of little consequence either to individuals or to Government. Nations are not primarily ruled by laws; less by violence. Whatever original energy may be supposed either in force or regulation, the operation of both is, in truth, merely instrumental. Nations are governed by the same methods, and on the same principles, by which an individual without authority is often able to govern those who are his equals or his superiors, by a knowledge of their temper, and by a judicious management of it; I mean, when public affairs are steadily and quietly conducted: not when Government is nothing but a continued scuffle between the magistrate and the multitude, in which sometimes the one and sometimes the other is uppermost—in which they alternately yield and prevail, in a series of contemptible victories and scandalous submissions. The temper of the people amongst whom he presides ought therefore to be the first study of a statesman. And the knowledge of this temper it is by no means impossible for him to attain, if he has not an interest in being ignorant of what it is his duty to learn.

To complain of the age we live in, to murmur at the present possessors of power, to lament the past, to conceive extravagant hopes of the future, are the common dispositions of the greater part of mankind—indeed, the necessary effects of the ignorance and levity of the vulgar. Such complaints and humours have existed in all times; yet as all times have *not* been alike, true political sagacity manifests itself, in distinguishing that complaint which only characterises the general infirmity of human nature from those which are symptoms of the particular distemperature of our own air and season.

\* \* \* \* \*

Nobody, I believe, will consider it merely as the language of spleen or disappointment, if I say that there is something particularly alarming in the present conjuncture. There is hardly a man, in or out of power, who holds any other language. That Government is at once dreaded and contemned; that the laws are despoiled of all their respected and salutary terrors; that their inaction is a subject of ridicule, and their exertion of abhorrence; that rank, and office, and title, and all the solemn plausibilities of the world, have lost their reverence and effect; that our foreign politics are as much deranged as our domestic economy; that our dependencies are slackened in their affection, and loosened from their obedience; that we know neither how to yield nor how to enforce; that hardly anything above or below, abroad or at home, is sound and entire; but that disconnection and confusion, in offices, in parties, in families, in Parliament, in the nation, prevail beyond the disorders of any former time: these are facts universally admitted and lamented.

This state of things is the more extraordinary, because the great parties which formerly divided and agitated the kingdom are known to be in a manner entirely dissolved. No great external calamity has visited the nation; no pestilence or famine. We do not labour at present under any scheme of taxation new or oppressive in the quantity or in the mode. Nor are we engaged in unsuccessful war, in which our misfortunes might easily pervert our judgment, and our minds, sore from the loss of national glory, might feel every blow of fortune as a crime in Government.

\* \* \* \* \*

It is impossible that the cause of this strange distemper should not sometimes become a subject of discourse. It is a compliment due, and which I willingly pay, to those who administer our affairs, to take notice in the first place of their speculation. Our Ministers are of opinion that the increase of our trade and manufactures, that our growth by colonisation and by conquest, have concurred to accumulate immense wealth in the hands of some individuals; and this again being dispersed amongst the people, has rendered them universally proud, ferocious, and ungovernable; that the insolence of some from their enormous wealth, and the boldness of others from a guilty poverty, have rendered them capable of the most atrocious attempts; so that they have trampled upon all subordination, and violently borne down the unarmed laws of a free Government—barriers too feeble against the fury of a populace so fierce and licentious as ours. They contend that no adequate provocation has been given for so spreading a discontent, our affairs having been conducted throughout with remarkable temper and consummate wisdom. The wicked industry of some libellers, joined to the intrigues of a few disappointed politicians, have, in their opinion, been able to produce this unnatural ferment in the nation.

Nothing indeed can be more unnatural than the present convulsions of this country, if the above account be a true one. I confess I shall assent to it with great reluctance, and only on the compulsion of the clearest and firmest proofs; because their account resolves itself into this short but discouraging proposition, "That we have a very good Ministry, but that we are a very bad people;" that we set ourselves to bite the hand that feeds us; that with a malignant insanity we oppose the measures, and ungratefully vilify the persons, of those whose sole object is our own peace and prosperity. If a few puny libellers, acting under a knot of factious politicians, without virtue, parts, or character (such they are constantly represented by these gentlemen), are sufficient to excite this disturbance, very perverse must be the disposition of that people amongst whom such a disturbance can be excited by such means. It is besides no small aggravation of the public misfortune that the disease, on this hypothesis, appears to be without remedy. If the wealth of the nation be the cause of its turbulence, I imagine it is not proposed to introduce poverty as a constable to keep the peace. If our dominions abroad are the roots which feed all this rank luxuriance of sedition, it is not intended to cut them off in order to famish the fruit. If our liberty has enfeebled the executive power, there is no design, I hope, to call in the aid of despotism to fill up the deficiencies of law. Whatever may be intended, these things are not yet professed. We seem therefore to be driven to absolute despair, for we have no other materials to work upon but those out of which God has been pleased to form the inhabitants of this island. If these be radically and essentially vicious, all that can be said is that those men are very unhappy to whose fortune or duty it falls to administer the affairs of this untoward people. I hear it indeed sometimes asserted that a steady perseverance in the present measures, and a rigorous punishment of those who oppose them, will in course of time infallibly put an end to these disorders. But this, in my opinion, is said without much observation of our present disposition, and without any knowledge at all of the general nature of mankind. If the matter of which this nation is composed be so very fermentable as these gentlemen describe it, leaven never will be wanting to work it up, as long as discontent, revenge, and ambition have existence in the world. Particular punishments are the cure for accidental distempers in the State; they inflame rather than allay those heats which arise from the settled mismanagement of the Government, or from a natural ill disposition in the people. It is of the utmost moment not to make mistakes in the use of strong measures, and firmness is then only a virtue when it accompanies the most perfect wisdom. In truth, inconstancy is a sort of natural corrective of folly and ignorance.

I am not one of those who think that the people are never in the wrong. They have been so, frequently and outrageously, both in other countries and in this. But I do say that in all disputes between them and their rulers the presumption is at least upon a par in favour of the people. Experience may perhaps justify me in going further. When popular discontents have been very prevalent, it may well be affirmed and supported that there has been generally something found amiss in the constitution or in the conduct of Government. The people have no interest in disorder. When they do wrong, it is their error, and not their crime. But with the governing part of the State it is far otherwise. They certainly may act ill by design, as well as by mistake. "Les révolutions qui arrivent dans les grands états ne sont point un effect du hasard, ni du caprice des peuples. Rien ne révolte les grands d'un royaume comme un Gouvernoment foible et dérangé. Pour la populace, ce n'est jamais par envie d'attaquer qu'elle se soulève, mais par impatience de souffrir." These are the words of a great man, of a Minister of State, and a zealous assertor of Monarchy. They are applied to the system of favouritism which was adopted by Henry the Third of France, and to the dreadful consequences it produced. What he says of revolutions is equally true of all great disturbances. If this presumption in favour of the subjects against the trustees of power be not the more probable, I am sure it is the more comfortable speculation, because it is more easy to change an Administration than to reform a people.

\* \* \* \* \*

Upon a supposition, therefore, that, in the opening of the cause, the presumptions stand equally balanced between the parties, there seems sufficient ground to entitle any person to a fair hearing who attempts some other scheme besides that easy one which is fashionable in some fashionable companies, to account for the present discontents. It is not to be argued that we endure no grievance, because our grievances are not of the same sort with those under which we laboured formerly—not precisely those which we bore from the Tudors, or vindicated on the Stuarts. A great change has taken place in the affairs of this country. For in the silent lapse of events as material alterations have been insensibly brought about in the policy and character of governments and nations as those which have been marked by the tumult of public revolutions.

It is very rare indeed for men to be wrong in their feelings concerning public misconduct; as rare to be right in their speculation upon the cause of it. I have constantly observed that the generality of people are fifty years, at least, behindhand in their politics. There are but very few who are capable of comparing and digesting what passes before their eyes at different times and occasions, so as to form the whole into a distinct system. But in books everything is settled for them, without the exertion of any considerable diligence or sagacity. For which reason men are wise with but little reflection, and good with little self-denial, in the business of all times except their own. We are very uncorrupt and tolerably enlightened judges of the transactions of past ages; where no passions deceive, and where the whole train of circumstances, from the trifling cause to the tragical event, is set in an orderly series before us. Few are the partisans of departed tyranny; and to be a Whig on the business of a hundred years ago is very consistent with every advantage of present servility. This retrospective wisdom and historical patriotism are things of wonderful convenience, and serve admirably to reconcile the old quarrel between speculation and practice. Many a stern republican, after gorging himself with a full feast of admiration of the Grecian commonwealths and of our true Saxon constitution, and discharging all the splendid bile of his virtuous indignation on King John and King James, sits down perfectly satisfied to the coarsest work and homeliest job of the day he lives in. I believe there was no professed admirer of Henry the Eighth among the instruments of the last King James; nor in the court of Henry the Eighth was there, I dare say, to be found a single advocate for the favourites of Richard the Second.

No complaisance to our Court, or to our age, can make me believe nature to be so changed but that public liberty will be among us, as among our ancestors, obnoxious to some person or other, and that opportunities will be furnished for attempting, at least, some alteration to the prejudice of our constitution. These attempts will naturally vary in their mode, according to times and circumstances. For ambition, though it has ever the same general views, has not at all times the same means, nor the same particular objects. A great deal of the furniture of ancient tyranny is worn to rags; the rest is entirely out of fashion. Besides, there are few statesmen so very clumsy and awkward in their business as to fall into the identical snare which has proved fatal to their predecessors. When an arbitrary imposition is attempted upon the subject, undoubtedly it will not bear on its forehead the name of *Ship-money*. There is no danger that an extension of the *Forest laws* should be the chosen mode of oppression in this age. And when we hear any instance of ministerial rapacity to the prejudice of the rights of private life, it will certainly not be the exaction of two hundred pullets, from a woman of fashion, for leave to lie with her own husband.

Every age has its own manners, and its politics dependent upon them; and the same attempts will not be made against a constitution fully formed and matured, that were used to destroy it in the cradle, or to resist its growth during its infancy.

Against the being of Parliament, I am satisfied, no designs have ever been entertained since the Revolution. Every one must perceive that it is strongly the interest of the Court to have some second cause interposed between the Ministers and the people. The gentlemen of the House of Commons have an interest equally strong in sustaining the part of that intermediate cause. However they may hire out the *usufruct* of their voices, they never will part with the *fee and inheritance*. Accordingly those who have been of the most known devotion to the will and pleasure of a Court, have at the same time been most forward in asserting a high authority in the House of Commons. When they knew who were to use that authority, and how it was to be employed, they thought it never could be carried too far. It must be always the wish of an unconstitutional statesman, that a House of Commons who are entirely dependent upon him, should have every right of the people entirely dependent upon their pleasure. It was soon discovered that the forms of a free, and the ends of an arbitrary Government, were things not altogether incompatible.

The power of the Crown, almost dead and rotten as Prerogative, has grown up anew, with much more strength, and far less odium, under the name of Influence. An influence which operated without noise and without violence; an influence which converted the very antagonist into the instrument of power; which contained in itself a perpetual principle of growth and renovation; and which the distresses and the prosperity of the country equally tended to augment, was an admirable substitute for a prerogative that, being only the offspring of antiquated prejudices, had moulded in its original stamina irresistible principles of decay and dissolution. The ignorance of the people is a bottom but for a temporary system; the interest of active men in the State is a foundation perpetual and infallible. However, some circumstances, arising, it must be confessed, in a great degree from accident, prevented the effects of this influence for a long time from breaking out in a manner capable of exciting any serious apprehensions. Although Government was strong and flourished exceedingly, the *Court* had drawn far less advantage than one would imagine from this great source of power.

\* \* \* \* \*

At the Revolution, the Crown, deprived, for the ends of the Revolution itself, of many prerogatives, was found too weak to struggle against all the difficulties which pressed so new and unsettled a Government. The Court was obliged therefore to delegate a part of its powers to men of such interest as could support, and of such fidelity as would adhere to, its establishment. Such men were able to draw in a greater number to a concurrence in the common defence. This connection, necessary at first, continued long after convenient; and properly conducted might indeed, in all situations, be a useful instrument of Government. At the same time, through the intervention of men of popular weight and character, the people possessed a security for their just proportion of importance in the State. But as the title to the Crown grew stronger by long possession, and by the constant increase of its influence, these helps have of late seemed to certain persons no better than incumbrances. The powerful managers for Government were not sufficiently submissive to the pleasure of the possessors of immediate and personal favour, sometimes from a confidence in their own strength, natural and acquired; sometimes from a fear of offending their friends, and weakening that lead in the country, which gave them a consideration independent of the Court. Men acted as if the Court could receive, as well as confer, an obligation. The influence of Government, thus divided in appearance between the Court and the leaders of parties, became in many cases an accession rather to the popular than to the royal scale; and some part of that influence, which would otherwise have been possessed as in a sort of mortmain and unalienable domain, returned again to the great ocean from whence it arose, and circulated among the people. This method therefore of governing by men of great natural interest or great acquired consideration, was viewed in a very invidious light by the true lovers of absolute monarchy. It is the nature of despotism to abhor power held by any means but its own momentary pleasure; and to annihilate all intermediate situations between boundless strength on its own part, and total debility on the part of the people.

To get rid of all this intermediate and independent importance, and *to secure to the Court the unlimited and uncontrolled use of its own vast influence, under the sole direction of its own private favour*, has for some years past been the great object of policy. If this were compassed, the influence of the Crown must of course produce all the effects which the most sanguine partisans of the Court could possibly desire. Government might then be carried on without any concurrence on the part of the people; without any attention to the dignity of the greater, or to the affections of the lower sorts. A new project was therefore devised by a certain set of intriguing men, totally different from the system of Administration which had prevailed since the accession of the House of Brunswick. This project, I have heard, was first conceived by some persons in the Court of Frederick, Prince of Wales.

The earliest attempt in the execution of this design was to set up for Minister a person, in rank indeed respectable, and very ample in fortune; but who, to the moment of this vast and sudden elevation, was little known or considered in the kingdom. To him the whole nation was to yield an immediate and implicit submission. But whether it was from want of firmness to bear up against the first opposition, or that things were not yet fully ripened, or that this method was not found the most eligible, that idea was soon abandoned. The instrumental part of the project was a little altered, to accommodate it to the time, and to bring things more gradually and more surely to the one great end proposed.

The first part of the reformed plan was to draw *a line which should separate the Court from the Ministry.* Hitherto these names had been looked upon as synonymous; but, for the future, Court and Administration were to be considered as things totally distinct. By this operation, two systems of Administration were to be formed: one which should be in the real secret and confidence; the other merely ostensible, to perform the official and executory duties of Government. The latter were alone to be responsible; whilst the real advisers, who enjoyed all the power, were effectually removed from all the danger.

Secondly, *a party under these leaders was to be formed in favour of the Court against the Ministry:* this party was to have a large share in the emoluments of Government, and to hold it totally separate from, and independent of, ostensible Administration.

The third point, and that on which the success of the whole scheme ultimately depended, was *to bring Parliament to an acquiescence in this project.* Parliament was therefore to be taught by degrees a total indifference to the persons, rank, influence, abilities, connections, and character of the Ministers of the Crown. By means of a discipline, on which I shall say more hereafter, that body was to be habituated to the most opposite interests, and the most discordant politics. All connections and dependencies among subjects were to be entirely dissolved. As hitherto business had gone through the hands of leaders of Whigs or Tories, men of talents to conciliate the people, and to engage their confidence, now the method was to be altered; and the lead was to be given to men of no sort of consideration or credit in the country. This want of natural importance was to be their very title to delegated power. Members of parliament were to be hardened into an insensibility to pride as well as to duty. Those high and haughty sentiments, which are the great support of independence, were to be let down gradually. Point of honour and precedence were no more to be regarded in Parliamentary decorum than in a Turkish army. It was to be avowed, as a constitutional maxim, that the King might appoint one of his footmen, or one of your footmen, for Minister; and that he ought to be, and that he would be, as well followed as the first name for rank or wisdom in the nation. Thus Parliament was to look on, as if perfectly unconcerned while a cabal of the closet and back-stairs was substituted in the place of a national Administration.

With such a degree of acquiescence, any measure of any Court might well be deemed thoroughly secure. The capital objects, and by much the most flattering characteristics of arbitrary power, would be obtained. Everything would be drawn from its holdings in the country to the personal favour and inclination of the Prince. This favour would be the sole introduction to power, and the only tenure by which it was to be held: so that no person looking towards another, and all looking towards the Court, it was impossible but that the motive which solely influenced every man's hopes must come in time to govern every man's conduct; till at last the servility became universal, in spite of the dead letter of any laws or institutions whatsoever.

How it should happen that any man could be tempted to venture upon such a project of Government, may at first view appear surprising. But the fact is that opportunities very inviting to such an attempt have offered; and the scheme itself was not destitute of some arguments, not wholly unplausible, to recommend it. These opportunities and these arguments, the use that has been made of both, the plan for carrying this new scheme of government into execution, and the effects which it has produced, are in my opinion worthy of our serious consideration.

His Majesty came to the throne of these kingdoms with more advantages than any of his predecessors since the Revolution. Fourth in descent, and third in succession of his Royal family, even the zealots of hereditary right, in him, saw something to flatter their favourite prejudices; and to justify a transfer of their attachments, without a change in their principles. The person and cause of the Pretender were become contemptible; his title disowned throughout Europe, his party disbanded in England. His Majesty came indeed to the inheritance of a mighty war; but, victorious in every part of the globe, peace was always in his power, not to negotiate, but to dictate. No foreign habitudes or attachments withdrew him from the cultivation of his power at home. His revenue for the Civil establishment, fixed (as it was then thought) at a large, but definite sum, was ample, without being invidious; his influence, by additions from conquest, by an augmentation of debt, by an increase of military and naval establishment, much strengthened and extended. And coming to the throne in the prime and full vigour of youth, as from affection there was a strong dislike, so from dread there seemed to be a general averseness from giving anything like offence to a monarch against whose resentment opposition could not look for a refuge in any sort of reversionary hope.

These singular advantages inspired his Majesty only with a more ardent desire to preserve unimpaired the spirit of that national freedom to which he owed a situation so full of glory. But to others it suggested sentiments of a very different nature. They thought they now beheld an opportunity (by a certain sort of statesman never long undiscovered or unemployed) of drawing to themselves, by the aggrandisement of a Court faction, a degree of power which they could never hope to derive from natural influence or from honourable service; and which it was impossible they could hold with the least security, whilst the system of Administration rested upon its former bottom. In order to facilitate the execution of their design, it was necessary to make many alterations in political arrangement, and a signal change in the opinions, habits, and connections of the greater part of those who at that time acted in public.

In the first place, they proceeded gradually, but not slowly, to destroy everything of strength which did not derive its principal nourishment from the immediate pleasure of the Court. The greatest weight of popular opinion and party connection were then with the Duke of Newcastle and Mr. Pitt. Neither of these held his importance by the *new tenure* of the Court; they were not, therefore, thought to be so proper as others for the services which were required by that tenure. It happened very favourably for the new system, that under a forced coalition there rankled an incurable alienation and disgust between the parties which composed the Administration. Mr. Pitt was first attacked. Not satisfied with removing him from power, they endeavoured by various artifices to ruin his character. The other party seemed rather pleased to get rid of so oppressive a support; not perceiving that their own fall was prepared by his, and involved in it. Many other reasons prevented them from daring to look their true situation in the face. To the great Whig families it was extremely disagreeable, and seemed almost unnatural, to oppose the Administration of a Prince of the House of Brunswick. Day after day they hesitated, and doubted, and lingered, expecting that other counsels would take place; and were slow to be persuaded that all which had been done by the Cabal was the effect, not of humour, but of system. It was more strongly and evidently the interest of the new Court faction to get rid of the great Whig connections than to destroy Mr. Pitt. The power of that gentleman was vast indeed, and merited; but it was in a great degree personal, and therefore transient. Theirs was rooted in the country. For, with a good deal less of popularity, they possessed a far more natural and fixed influence. Long possession of Government; vast property; obligations of favours given and received; connection of office; ties of blood, of alliance, of friendship (things at that time supposed of some force); the name of Whig, dear to the majority of the people; the zeal early begun and steadily continued to the Royal Family; all these together formed a body of power in the nation, which was criminal and devoted. The great ruling principle of the Cabal, and that which animated and harmonised all their proceedings, how various soever they may have been, was to signify to the world that the Court would proceed upon its own proper forces only; and that the pretence of bringing any other into its service was an affront to it, and not a support. Therefore when the chiefs were removed, in order to go to the root, the whole party was put under a proscription, so general and severe as to take their hard-earned bread from the lowest officers, in a manner which had never been known before, even in general revolutions. But it was thought necessary effectually to destroy all dependencies but one, and to show an example of the firmness and rigour with which the new system was to be supported.

Thus for the time were pulled down, in the persons of the Whig leaders and of Mr. Pitt (in spite of the services of the one at the accession of the Royal Family, and the recent services of the other in the war), the *two only securities for the importance of the people: power arising from popularity, and power arising from connection.* Here and there indeed a few individuals were left standing, who gave security for their total estrangement from the odious principles of party connection and personal attachment; and it must be confessed that most of them have religiously kept their faith. Such a change could not, however, be made without a mighty shock to Government.

To reconcile the minds of the people to all these movements, principles correspondent to them had been preached up with great zeal. Every one must remember that the Cabal set out with the most astonishing prudery, both moral and political. Those who in a few months after soused over head and ears into the deepest and dirtiest pits of corruption, cried out violently against the indirect practices in the electing and managing of Parliaments, which had formerly prevailed. This marvellous abhorrence which the Court had suddenly taken to all influence, was not only circulated in conversation through the kingdom, but pompously announced to the public, with many other extraordinary things, in a pamphlet which had all the appearance of a manifesto preparatory to some considerable enterprise. Throughout, it was a satire, though in terms managed and decent enough, on the politics of the former reign. It was indeed written with no small art and address.

In this piece appeared the first dawning of the new system; there first appeared the idea (then only in speculation) of *separating the Court from the Administration*; of carrying everything from national connection to personal regards; and of forming a regular party for that purpose, under the name of *King's men.*

To recommend this system to the people, a perspective view of the Court, gorgeously painted, and finely illuminated from within, was exhibited to the gaping multitude. Party was to be totally done away, with all its evil works. Corruption was to be cast down from Court, as *Atè* was from heaven. Power was thenceforward to be the chosen residence of public spirit; and no one was to be supposed under any sinister influence, except those who had the misfortune to be in disgrace at Court, which was to stand in lieu of all vices and all corruptions. A scheme of perfection to be realised in a Monarchy, far beyond the visionary Republic of Plato. The whole scenery was exactly disposed to captivate those good souls, whose credulous morality is so invaluable a treasure to crafty politicians. Indeed, there was wherewithal to charm everybody, except those few who are not much pleased with professions of supernatural virtue, who know of what stuff such professions are made, for what purposes they are designed, and in what they are sure constantly to end. Many innocent gentlemen, who had been talking prose all their lives without knowing anything of the matter, began at last to open their eyes upon their own merits, and to attribute their not having been Lords of the Treasury and Lords of Trade many years before merely to the prevalence of party, and to the Ministerial power, which had frustrated the good intentions of the Court in favour of their abilities. Now was the time to unlock the sealed fountain of Royal bounty, which had been infamously monopolised and huckstered, and to let it flow at large upon the whole people. The time was come to restore Royalty to its original splendour. *Mettre le Roy hors de page*, became a sort of watchword. And it was constantly in the mouths of all the runners of the Court, that nothing could preserve the balance of the constitution from being overturned by the rabble, or by a faction of the nobility, but to free the Sovereign effectually from that Ministerial tyranny under which the Royal dignity had been oppressed in the person of his Majesty's grandfather.

These were some of the many artifices used to reconcile the people to the great change which was made in the persons who composed the Ministry, and the still greater which was made and avowed in its constitution. As to individuals, other methods were employed with them, in order so thoroughly to disunite every party, and even every family, that *no concert, order, or effect, might appear in any future opposition.* And in this manner an Administration without connection with the people, or with one another, was first put in possession of Government. What good consequences followed from it, we have all seen; whether with regard to virtue, public or private; to the ease and happiness of the Sovereign; or to the real strength of Government. But as so much stress was then laid on the necessity of this new project, it will not be amiss to take a view of the effects of this Royal servitude and vile durance, which was so deplored in the reign of the late Monarch, and was so carefully to be avoided in the reign of his successor. The effects were these.

In times full of doubt and danger to his person and family, George the Second maintained the dignity of his Crown connected with the liberty of his people, not only unimpaired, but improved, for the space of thirty-three years. He overcame a dangerous rebellion, abetted by foreign force, and raging in the heart of his kingdoms; and thereby destroyed the seeds of all future rebellion that could arise upon the same principle. He carried the glory, the power, the commerce of England, to a height unknown even to this renowned nation in the times of its greatest prosperity: and he left his succession resting on the true and only true foundation of all national and all regal greatness; affection at home, reputation abroad, trust in allies, terror in rival nations. The most ardent lover of his country cannot wish for Great Britain a happier fate than to continue as she was then left. A people emulous as we are in affection to our present Sovereign, know not how to form a prayer to Heaven for a greater blessing upon his virtues, or a higher state of felicity and glory, than that he should live, and should reign, and, when Providence ordains it, should die, exactly like his illustrious predecessor.

A great Prince may be obliged (though such a thing cannot happen very often) to sacrifice his private inclination to his public interest. A wise Prince will not think that such a restraint implies a condition of servility; and truly, if such was the condition of the last reign, and the effects were also such as we have described, we ought, no less for the sake of the Sovereign whom we love, than for our own, to hear arguments convincing indeed, before we depart from the maxims of that reign, or fly in the face of this great body of strong and recent experience.

One of the principal topics which was then, and has been since, much employed by that political school, is an effectual terror of the growth of an aristocratic power, prejudicial to the rights of the Crown, and the balance of the constitution. Any new powers exercised in the House of Lords, or in the House of Commons, or by the Crown, ought certainly to excite the vigilant and anxious jealousy of a free people. Even a new and unprecedented course of action in the whole Legislature, without great and evident reason, may be a subject of just uneasiness. I will not affirm, that there may not have lately appeared in the House of Lords a disposition to some attempts derogatory to the legal rights of the subject. If any such have really appeared, they have arisen, not from a power properly aristocratic, but from the same influence which is charged with having excited attempts of a similar nature in the House of Commons; which House, if it should have been betrayed into an unfortunate quarrel with its constituents, and involved in a charge of the very same nature, could have neither power nor inclination to repel such attempts in others. Those attempts in the House of Lords can no more be called aristocratic proceedings, than the proceedings with regard to the county of Middlesex in the House of Commons can with any sense be called democratical.

It is true, that the Peers have a great influence in the kingdom, and in every part of the public concerns. While they are men of property, it is impossible to prevent it, except by such means as must prevent all property from its natural operation: an event not easily to be compassed, while property is power; nor by any means to be wished, while the least notion exists of the method by which the spirit of liberty acts, and of the means by which it is preserved. If any particular Peers, by their uniform, upright, constitutional conduct, by their public and their private virtues, have acquired an influence in the country; the people on whose favour that influence depends, and from whom it arose, will never be duped into an opinion, that such greatness in a Peer is the despotism of an aristocracy, when they know and feel it to be the effect and pledge of their own importance.

I am no friend to aristocracy, in the sense at least in which that word is usually understood. If it were not a bad habit to moot cases on the supposed ruin of the constitution, I should be free to declare, that if it must perish, I would rather by far see it resolved into any other form, than lost in that austere and insolent domination. But, whatever my dislikes may be, my fears are not upon that quarter. The question, on the influence of a Court, and of a Peerage, is not, which of the two dangers is the most eligible, but which is the most imminent. He is but a poor observer, who has not seen, that the generality of Peers, far from supporting themselves in a state of independent greatness, are but too apt to fall into an oblivion of their proper dignity, and to run headlong into an abject servitude. Would to God it were true, that the fault of our Peers were too much spirit! It is worthy of some observation, that these gentlemen, so jealous of aristocracy, make no complaints of the power of those peers (neither few nor inconsiderable) who are always in the train of a Court, and whose whole weight must be considered as a portion of the settled influence of the Crown. This is all safe and right; but if some Peers (I am very sorry they are not as many as they ought to be) set themselves, in the great concern of Peers and Commons, against a back-stairs influence and clandestine government, then the alarm begins; then the constitution is in danger of being forced into an aristocracy.

I rest a little the longer on this Court topic, because it was much insisted upon at the time of the great change, and has been since frequently revived by many of the agents of that party: for, whilst they are terrifying the great and opulent with the horrors of mob-government, they are by other managers attempting (though hitherto with little success) to alarm the people with a phantom of tyranny in the Nobles. All this is done upon their favourite principle of disunion, of sowing jealousies amongst the different orders of the State, and of disjointing the natural strength of the kingdom; that it may be rendered incapable of resisting the sinister designs of wicked men, who have engrossed the Royal power.

\* \* \* \* \*

Thus much of the topics chosen by the courtiers to recommend their system; it will be necessary to open a little more at large the nature of that party which was formed for its support. Without this, the whole would have been no better than a visionary amusement, like the scheme of Harrington's political club, and not a business in which the nation had a real concern. As a powerful party, and a party constructed on a new principle, it is a very inviting object of curiosity.

It must be remembered, that since the Revolution, until the period we are speaking of, the influence of the Crown had been always employed in supporting the Ministers of State, and in carrying on the public business according to their opinions. But the party now in question is formed upon a very different idea. It is to intercept the favour, protection, and confidence of the Crown in the passage to its Ministers; it is to come between them and their importance in Parliament; it is to separate them from all their natural and acquired dependencies; it is intended as the control, not the support, of Administration. The machinery of this system is perplexed in its movements, and false in its principle. It is formed on a supposition that the King is something external to his government; and that he may be honoured and aggrandised, even by its debility and disgrace. The plan proceeds expressly on the idea of enfeebling the regular executory power. It proceeds on the idea of weakening the State in order to strengthen the Court. The scheme depending entirely on distrust, on disconnection, on mutability by principle, on systematic weakness in every particular member; it is impossible that the total result should be substantial strength of any kind.

As a foundation of their scheme, the Cabal have established a sort of *Rota* in the Court. All sorts of parties, by this means, have been brought into Administration, from whence few have had the good fortune to escape without disgrace; none at all without considerable losses. In the beginning of each arrangement no professions of confidence and support are wanting, to induce the leading men to engage. But while the Ministers of the day appear in all the pomp and pride of power, while they have all their canvas spread out to the wind, and every sail filled with the fair and prosperous gale of Royal favour, in a short time they find, they know not how, a current, which sets directly against them; which prevents all progress, and even drives them backwards. They grow ashamed and mortified in a situation, which, by its vicinity to power, only serves to remind them the more strongly of their insignificance. They are obliged either to execute the orders of their inferiors, or to see themselves opposed by the natural instruments of their office. With the loss of their dignity, they lose their temper. In their turn they grow troublesome to that Cabal, which, whether it supports or opposes, equally disgraces and equally betrays them. It is soon found necessary to get rid of the heads of Administration; but it is of the heads only. As there always are many rotten members belonging to the best connections, it is not hard to persuade several to continue in office without their leaders. By this means the party goes out much thinner than it came in; and is only reduced in strength by its temporary possession of power. Besides, if by accident, or in course of changes, that power should be recovered, the Junto have thrown up a retrenchment of these carcases, which may serve to cover themselves in a day of danger. They conclude, not unwisely, that such rotten members will become the first objects of disgust and resentment to their ancient connections.

They contrive to form in the outward Administration two parties at the least; which, whilst they are tearing one another to pieces, are both competitors for the favour and protection of the Cabal; and, by their emulation, contribute to throw everything more and more into the hands of the interior managers.

A Minister of State will sometimes keep himself totally estranged from all his colleagues; will differ from them in their counsels, will privately traverse, and publicly oppose, their measures. He will, however, continue in his employment. Instead of suffering any mark of displeasure, he will be distinguished by an unbounded profusion of Court rewards and caresses; because he does what is expected, and all that is expected, from men in office. He helps to keep some form of Administration in being, and keeps it at the same time as weak and divided as possible.

However, we must take care not to be mistaken, or to imagine that such persons have any weight in their opposition. When, by them, Administration is convinced of its insignificancy, they are soon to be convinced of their own. They never are suffered to succeed in their opposition. They and the world are to be satisfied, that neither office, nor authority, nor property, nor ability, eloquence, counsel, skill, or union, are of the least importance; but that the mere influence of the Court, naked of all support, and destitute of all management, is abundantly sufficient for all its own purposes.

When any adverse connection is to be destroyed, the Cabal seldom appear in the work themselves. They find out some person of whom the party entertains a high opinion. Such a person they endeavour to delude with various pretences. They teach him first to distrust, and then to quarrel with his friends; among whom, by the same arts, they excite a similar diffidence of him; so that in this mutual fear and distrust, he may suffer himself to be employed as the instrument in the change which is brought about. Afterwards they are sure to destroy him in his turn; by setting up in his place some person in whom he had himself reposed the greatest confidence, and who serves to carry on a considerable part of his adherents.

When such a person has broke in this manner with his connections, he is soon compelled to commit some flagrant act of iniquitous personal hostility against some of them (such as an attempt to strip a particular friend of his family estate), by which the Cabal hope to render the parties utterly irreconcilable. In truth, they have so contrived matters, that people have a greater hatred to the subordinate instruments than to the principal movers.

As in destroying their enemies they make use of instruments not immediately belonging to their corps, so in advancing their own friends they pursue exactly the same method. To promote any of them to considerable rank or emolument, they commonly take care that the recommendation shall pass through the hands of the ostensible Ministry: such a recommendation might, however, appear to the world as some proof of the credit of Ministers, and some means of increasing their strength. To prevent this, the persons so advanced are directed in all companies, industriously to declare, that they are under no obligations whatsoever to Administration; that they have received their office from another quarter; that they are totally free and independent.

When the Faction has any job of lucre to obtain, or of vengeance to perpetrate, their way is, to select, for the execution, those very persons to whose habits, friendships, principles, and declarations, such proceedings are publicly known to be the most adverse; at once to render the instruments the more odious, and therefore the more dependent, and to prevent the people from ever reposing a confidence in any appearance of private friendship, or public principle.

If the Administration seem now and then, from remissness, or from fear of making themselves disagreeable, to suffer any popular excesses to go unpunished, the Cabal immediately sets up some creature of theirs to raise a clamour against the Ministers, as having shamefully betrayed the dignity of Government. Then they compel the Ministry to become active in conferring rewards and honours on the persons who have been the instruments of their disgrace; and, after having first vilified them with the higher orders for suffering the laws to sleep over the licentiousness of the populace, they drive them (in order to make amends for their former inactivity) to some act of atrocious violence, which renders them completely abhorred by the people. They who remember the riots which attended the Middlesex Election; the opening of the present Parliament; and the transactions relative to Saint George's Fields, will not be at a loss for an application of these remarks.

That this body may be enabled to compass all the ends of its institution, its members are scarcely ever to aim at the high and responsible offices of the State. They are distributed with art and judgment through all the secondary, but efficient, departments of office, and through the households of all the branches of the Royal Family: so as on one hand to occupy all the avenues to the Throne; and on the other to forward or frustrate the execution of any measure, according to their own interests. For with the credit and support which they are known to have, though for the greater part in places which are only a genteel excuse for salary, they possess all the influence of the highest posts; and they dictate publicly in almost everything, even with a parade of superiority. Whenever they dissent (as it often happens) from their nominal leaders, the trained part of the Senate, instinctively in the secret, is sure to follow them; provided the leaders, sensible of their situation, do not of themselves recede in time from their most declared opinions. This latter is generally the case. It will not be conceivable to any one who has not seen it, what pleasure is taken by the Cabal in rendering these heads of office thoroughly contemptible and ridiculous. And when they are become so, they have then the best chance, for being well supported.

The members of the Court faction are fully indemnified for not holding places on the slippery heights of the kingdom, not only by the lead in all affairs, but also by the perfect security in which they enjoy less conspicuous, but very advantageous, situations. Their places are, in express legal tenure, or in effect, all of them for life. Whilst the first and most respectable persons in the kingdom are tossed about like tennis balls, the sport of a blind and insolent caprice, no Minister dares even to cast an oblique glance at the lowest of their body. If an attempt be made upon one of this corps, immediately he flies to sanctuary, and pretends to the most inviolable of all promises. No conveniency of public arrangement is available to remove any one of them from the specific situation he holds; and the slightest attempt upon one of them, by the most powerful Minister, is a certain preliminary to his own destruction.

Conscious of their independence, they bear themselves with a lofty air to the exterior Ministers. Like Janissaries, they derive a kind of freedom from the very condition of their servitude. They may act just as they please; provided they are true to the great ruling principle of their institution. It is, therefore, not at all wonderful, that people should be so desirous of adding themselves to that body, in which they may possess and reconcile satisfactions the most alluring, and seemingly the most contradictory; enjoying at once all the spirited pleasure of independence, and all the gross lucre and fat emoluments of servitude.

Here is a sketch, though a slight one, of the constitution, laws, and policy, of this new Court corporation. The name by which they choose to distinguish themselves, is that of *King's men*, or the *King's friends*, by an invidious exclusion of the rest of his Majesty's most loyal and affectionate subjects. The whole system, comprehending the exterior and interior Administrations, is commonly called, in the technical language of the Court, *Double Cabinet*; in French or English, as you choose to pronounce it.

Whether all this be a vision of a distracted brain, or the invention of a malicious heart, or a real faction in the country, must be judged by the appearances which things have worn for eight years past. Thus far I am certain, that there is not a single public man, in or out of office, who has not, at some time or other, borne testimony to the truth of what I have now related. In particular, no persons have been more strong in their assertions, and louder and more indecent in their complaints, than those who compose all the exterior part of the present Administration; in whose time that faction has arrived at such a height of power, and of boldness in the use of it, as may, in the end, perhaps bring about its total destruction.

It is true, that about four years ago, during the administration of the Marquis of Rockingham, an attempt was made to carry on Government without their concurrence. However, this was only a transient cloud; they were hid but for a moment; and their constellation blazed out with greater brightness, and a far more vigorous influence, some time after it was blown over. An attempt was at that time made (but without any idea of proscription) to break their corps, to discountenance their doctrines, to revive connections of a different kind, to restore the principles and policy of the Whigs, to reanimate the cause of Liberty by Ministerial countenance; and then for the first time were men seen attached in office to every principle they had maintained in opposition. No one will doubt, that such men were abhorred and violently opposed by the Court faction, and that such a system could have but a short duration.

It may appear somewhat affected, that in so much discourse upon this extraordinary party, I should say so little of the Earl of Bute, who is the supposed head of it. But this was neither owing to affectation nor inadvertence. I have carefully avoided the introduction of personal reflections of any kind. Much the greater part of the topics which have been used to blacken this nobleman are either unjust or frivolous. At best, they have a tendency to give the resentment of this bitter calamity a wrong direction, and to turn a public grievance into a mean personal, or a dangerous national, quarrel. Where there is a regular scheme of operations carried on, it is the system, and not any individual person who acts in it, that is truly dangerous. This system has not risen solely from the ambition of Lord Bute, but from the circumstances which favoured it, and from an indifference to the constitution which had been for some time growing among our gentry. We should have been tried with it, if the Earl of Bute had never existed; and it will want neither a contriving head nor active members, when the Earl of Bute exists no longer. It is not, therefore, to rail at Lord Bute, but firmly to embody against this Court party and its practices, which can afford us any prospect of relief in our present condition.

Another motive induces me to put the personal consideration of Lord Bute wholly out of the question. He communicates very little in a direct manner with the greater part of our men of business. This has never been his custom. It is enough for him that he surrounds them with his creatures. Several imagine, therefore, that they have a very good excuse for doing all the work of this faction, when they have no personal connection with Lord Bute. But whoever becomes a party to an Administration, composed of insulated individuals, without faith plighted, tie, or common principle; an Administration constitutionally impotent, because supported by no party in the nation; he who contributes to destroy the connections of men and their trust in one another, or in any sort to throw the dependence of public counsels upon private will and favour, possibly may have nothing to do with the Earl of Bute. It matters little whether he be the friend or the enemy of that particular person. But let him be who or what he will, he abets a faction that is driving hard to the ruin of his country. He is sapping the foundation of its liberty, disturbing the sources of its domestic tranquillity, weakening its government over its dependencies, degrading it from all its importance in the system of Europe.

It is this unnatural infusion of a *system of Favouritism* into a Government which in a great part of its constitution is popular, that has raised the present ferment in the nation. The people, without entering deeply into its principles, could plainly perceive its effects, in much violence, in a great spirit of innovation, and a general disorder in all the functions of Government. I keep my eye solely on this system; if I speak of those measures which have arisen from it, it will be so far only as they illustrate the general scheme. This is the fountain of all those bitter waters of which, through a hundred different conducts, we have drunk until we are ready to burst. The discretionary power of the Crown in the formation of Ministry, abused by bad or weak men, has given rise to a system, which, without directly violating the letter of any law, operates against the spirit of the whole constitution.

A plan of Favouritism for our executory Government is essentially at variance with the plan of our Legislature. One great end undoubtedly of a mixed Government like ours, composed of Monarchy, and of controls, on the part of the higher people and the lower, is that the Prince shall not be able to violate the laws. This is useful indeed and fundamental. But this, even at first view, is no more than a negative advantage; an armour merely defensive. It is therefore next in order, and equal in importance, *that the discretionary powers which are necessarily vested in the Monarch, whether for the execution of the laws, or for the nomination to magistracy and office, or for conducting the affairs of peace and war, or for ordering the revenue, should all be exercised upon public principles and national grounds, and not on the likings or prejudices, the intrigues or policies of a Court.* This, I said, is equal in importance to the securing a Government according to law. The laws reach but a very little way. Constitute Government how you please, infinitely the greater part of it must depend upon the exercise of the powers which are left at large to the prudence and uprightness of Ministers of State. Even all the use and potency of the laws depends upon them. Without them, your Commonwealth is no better than a scheme upon paper; and not a living, active, effective constitution. It is possible, that through negligence, or ignorance, or design artfully conducted, Ministers may suffer one part of Government to languish, another to be perverted from its purposes: and every valuable interest of the country to fall into ruin and decay, without possibility of fixing any single act on which a criminal prosecution can be justly grounded. The due arrangement of men in the active part of the state, far from being foreign to the purposes of a wise Government, ought to be among its very first and dearest objects. When, therefore, the abettors of new system tell us, that between them and their opposers there is nothing but a struggle for power, and that therefore we are no-ways concerned in it; we must tell those who have the impudence to insult us in this manner, that, of all things, we ought to be the most concerned, who and what sort of men they are, that hold the trust of everything that is dear to us. Nothing can render this a point of indifference to the nation, but what must either render us totally desperate, or soothe us into the security of idiots. We must soften into a credulity below the milkiness of infancy, to think all men virtuous. We must be tainted with a malignity truly diabolical, to believe all the world to be equally wicked and corrupt. Men are in public life as in private—some good, some evil. The elevation of the one, and the depression of the other, are the first objects of all true policy. But that form of Government, which, neither in its direct institutions, nor in their immediate tendency, has contrived to throw its affairs into the most trustworthy hands, but has left its whole executory system to be disposed of agreeably to the uncontrolled pleasure of any one man, however excellent or virtuous, is a plan of polity defective not only in that member, but consequentially erroneous in every part of it.

In arbitrary Governments, the constitution of the Ministry follows the constitution of the Legislature. Both the Law and the Magistrate are the creatures of Will. It must be so. Nothing, indeed, will appear more certain, on any tolerable consideration of this matter, than that *every sort of Government ought to have its Administration correspondent to its Legislature.* If it should be otherwise, things must fall into a hideous disorder. The people of a free Commonwealth, who have taken such care that their laws should be the result of general consent, cannot be so senseless as to suffer their executory system to be composed of persons on whom they have no dependence, and whom no proofs of the public love and confidence have recommended to those powers, upon the use of which the very being of the State depends.

The popular election of magistrates, and popular disposition of rewards and honours, is one of the first advantages of a free State. Without it, or something equivalent to it, perhaps the people cannot long enjoy the substance of freedom; certainly none of the vivifying energy of good Government. The frame of our Commonwealth did not admit of such an actual election: but it provided as well, and (while the spirit of the constitution is preserved) better, for all the effects of it, than by the method of suffrage in any democratic State whatsoever. It had always, until of late, been held the first duty of Parliament *to refuse to support Government, until power was in the hands of persons who were acceptable to the people, or while factions predominated in the Court in which the nation had no confidence.* Thus all the good effects of popular election were supposed to be secured to us, without the mischiefs attending on perpetual intrigue, and a distinct canvass for every particular office throughout the body of the people. This was the most noble and refined part of our constitution. The people, by their representatives and grandees, were intrusted with a deliberative power in making laws; the King with the control of his negative. The King was intrusted with the deliberative choice and the election to office; the people had the negative in a Parliamentary refusal to support. Formerly this power of control was what kept Ministers in awe of Parliaments, and Parliaments in reverence with the people. If the use of this power of control on the system and persons of Administration is gone, everything is lost, Parliament and all. We may assure ourselves, that if Parliament will tamely see evil men take possession of all the strongholds of their country, and allow them time and means to fortify themselves, under a pretence of giving them a fair trial, and upon a hope of discovering, whether they will not be reformed by power, and whether their measures will not be better than their morals; such a Parliament will give countenance to their measures also, whatever that Parliament may pretend, and whatever those measures may be.

Every good political institution must have a preventive operation as well as a remedial. It ought to have a natural tendency to exclude bad men from Government, and not to trust for the safety of the State to subsequent punishment alone—punishment which has ever been tardy and uncertain, and which, when power is suffered in bad hands, may chance to fall rather on the injured than the criminal.

Before men are put forward into the great trusts of the State, they ought by their conduct to have obtained such a degree of estimation in their country as may be some sort of pledge and security to the public that they will not abuse those trusts. It is no mean security for a proper use of power, that a man has shown by the general tenor of his actions, that the affection, the good opinion, the confidence of his fellow-citizens have been among the principal objects of his life, and that he has owed none of the gradations of his power or fortune to a settled contempt or occasional forfeiture of their esteem.

That man who, before he comes into power, has no friends, or who, coming into power, is obliged to desert his friends, or who, losing it, has no friends to sympathise with him, he who has no sway among any part of the landed or commercial interest, but whose whole importance has begun with his office, and is sure to end with it, is a person who ought never to be suffered by a controlling Parliament, to continue in any of those situations which confer the lead and direction of all our public affairs; because such a man *has no connection with the sentiments and opinions of the people.*

Those knots or cabals of men who have got together, avowedly without any public principle, in order to sell their conjunct iniquity at the higher rate, and are therefore universally odious, ought never to be suffered to domineer in the State; because they have *no connection with the sentiments and opinions of the people.*

These are considerations which, in my opinion, enforce the necessity of having some better reason, in a free country and a free Parliament, for supporting the Ministers of the Crown, than that short one, *That the King has thought proper to appoint them.* There is something very courtly in this. But it is a principle pregnant with all sorts of mischief, in a constitution like ours, to turn the views of active men from the country to the Court. Whatever be the road to power, that is the road which will be trod. If the opinion of the country be of no use as a means of power or consideration, the qualities which usually procure that opinion will be no longer cultivated. And whether it will be right, in a State so popular in its constitution as ours, to leave ambition without popular motives, and to trust all to the operation of pure virtue in the minds of Kings and Ministers, and public men, must be submitted to the judgment and good sense of the people of England.

\* \* \* \* \*

Cunning men are here apt to break in, and, without directly controverting the principle, to raise objections from the difficulty under which the Sovereign labours to distinguish the genuine voice and sentiments of his people from the clamour of a faction, by which it is so easily counterfeited. The nation, they say, is generally divided into parties, with views and passions utterly irreconcilable. If the King should put his affairs into the hands of any one of them, he is sure to disgust the rest; if he select particular men from among them all, it is a hazard that he disgusts them all. Those who are left out, however divided before, will soon run into a body of opposition, which, being a collection of many discontents into one focus, will without doubt be hot and violent enough. Faction will make its cries resound through the nation, as if the whole were in an uproar, when by far the majority, and much the better part, will seem for awhile, as it were, annihilated by the quiet in which their virtue and moderation incline them to enjoy the blessings of Government. Besides that, the opinion of the mere vulgar is a miserable rule even with regard to themselves, on account of their violence and instability. So that if you were to gratify them in their humour to-day, that very gratification would be a ground of their dissatisfaction on the next. Now as all these rules of public opinion are to be collected with great difficulty, and to be applied with equal uncertainty as to the effect, what better can a King of England do than to employ such men as he finds to have views and inclinations most conformable to his own, who are least infected with pride and self-will, and who are least moved by such popular humours as are perpetually traversing his designs, and disturbing his service; trusting that when he means no ill to his people he will be supported in his appointments, whether he chooses to keep or to change, as his private judgment or his pleasure leads him? He will find a sure resource in the real weight and influence of the Crown, when it is not suffered to become an instrument in the hands of a faction.

I will not pretend to say that there is nothing at all in this mode of reasoning, because I will not assert that there is no difficulty in the art of government. Undoubtedly the very best Administration must encounter a great deal of opposition, and the very worst will find more support than it deserves. Sufficient appearances will never be wanting to those who have a mind to deceive themselves. It is a fallacy in constant use with those who would level all things, and confound right with wrong, to insist upon the inconveniences which are attached to every choice, without taking into consideration the different weight and consequence of those inconveniences. The question is not concerning absolute discontent or perfect satisfaction in Government, neither of which can be pure and unmixed at any time or upon any system. The controversy is about that degree of good-humour in the people, which may possibly be attained, and ought certainly to be looked for. While some politicians may be waiting to know whether the sense of every individual be against them, accurately distinguishing the vulgar from the better sort, drawing lines between the enterprises of a faction and the efforts of a people, they may chance to see the Government, which they are so nicely weighing, and dividing, and distinguishing, tumble to the ground in the midst of their wise deliberation. Prudent men, when so great an object as the security of Government, or even its peace, is at stake, will not run the risk of a decision which may be fatal to it. They who can read the political sky will seen a hurricane in a cloud no bigger than a hand at the very edge of the horizon, and will run into the first harbour. No lines can be laid down for civil or political wisdom. They are a matter incapable of exact definition. But, though no man can draw a stroke between the confines of day and night, yet light and darkness are upon the whole tolerably distinguishable. Nor will it be impossible for a Prince to find out such a mode of government, and such persons to administer it, as will give a great degree of content to his people, without any curious and anxious research for that abstract, universal, perfect harmony, which, while he is seeking, he abandons those means of ordinary tranquillity which are in his power without any research at all.

It is not more the duty than it is the interest of a Prince to aim at giving tranquillity to his Government. If those who advise him may have an interest in disorder and confusion. If the opinion of the people is against them, they will naturally wish that it should have no prevalence. Here it is that the people must on their part show themselves sensible of their own value. Their whole importance, in the first instance, and afterwards their whole freedom, is at stake. Their freedom cannot long survive their importance. Here it is that the natural strength of the kingdom, the great peers, the leading landed gentlemen, the opulent merchants and manufacturers, the substantial yeomanry, must interpose, to rescue their Prince, themselves, and their posterity.

We are at present at issue upon this point. We are in the great crisis of this contention, and the part which men take, one way or other, will serve to discriminate their characters and their principles. Until the matter is decided, the country will remain in its present confusion. For while a system of Administration is attempted, entirely repugnant to the genius of the people, and not conformable to the plan of their Government, everything must necessarily be disordered for a time, until this system destroys the constitution, or the constitution gets the better of this system.

There is, in my opinion, a peculiar venom and malignity in this political distemper beyond any that I have heard or read of. In former lines the projectors of arbitrary Government attacked only the liberties of their country, a design surely mischievous enough to have satisfied a mind of the most unruly ambition. But a system unfavourable to freedom may be so formed as considerably to exalt the grandeur of the State, and men may find in the pride and splendour of that prosperity some sort of consolation for the loss of their solid privileges. Indeed, the increase of the power of the State has often been urged by artful men, as a pretext for some abridgment of the public liberty. But the scheme of the junto under consideration not only strikes a palsy into every nerve of our free constitution, but in the same degree benumbs and stupefies the whole executive power, rendering Government in all its grand operations languid, uncertain, ineffective, making Ministers fearful of attempting, and incapable of executing, any useful plan of domestic arrangement, or of foreign politics. It tends to produce neither the security of a free Government, nor the energy of a Monarchy that is absolute. Accordingly, the Crown has dwindled away in proportion to the unnatural and turgid growth of this excrescence on the Court.

The interior Ministry are sensible that war is a situation which sets in its full light the value of the hearts of a people, and they well know that the beginning of the importance of the people must be the end of theirs. For this reason they discover upon all occasions the utmost fear of everything which by possibility may lead to such an event. I do not mean that they manifest any of that pious fear which is backward to commit the safety of the country to the dubious experiment of war. Such a fear, being the tender sensation of virtue, excited, as it is regulated, by reason, frequently shows itself in a seasonable boldness, which keeps danger at a distance, by seeming to despise it. Their fear betrays to the first glance of the eye its true cause and its real object. Foreign powers, confident in the knowledge of their character, have not scrupled to violate the most solemn treaties; and, in defiance of them, to make conquests in the midst of a general peace, and in the heart of Europe. Such was the conquest of Corsica, by the professed enemies of the freedom of mankind, in defiance of those who were formerly its professed defenders. We have had just claims upon the same powers— rights which ought to have been sacred to them as well as to us, as they had their origin in our lenity and generosity towards France and Spain in the day of their great humiliation. Such I call the ransom of Manilla, and the demand on France for the East India prisoners. But these powers put a just confidence in their resource of the double Cabinet. These demands (one of them, at least) are hastening fast towards an acquittal by prescription. Oblivion begins to spread her cobwebs over all our spirited remonstrances. Some of the most valuable branches of our trade are also on the point of perishing from the same cause. I do not mean those branches which bear without the hand of the vine-dresser; I mean those which the policy of treaties had formerly secured to us; I mean to mark and distinguish the trade of Portugal, the loss of which, and the power of the Cabal, have one and the same era.

If, by any chance, the Ministers who stand before the curtain possess or affect any spirit, it makes little or no impression. Foreign Courts and Ministers, who were among the first to discover and to profit by this invention of the *double Cabinet*, attended very little to their remonstrances. They know that those shadows of Ministers have nothing to do in the ultimate disposal of things. Jealousies and animosities are sedulously nourished in the outward Administration, and have been even considered as a *causa sine qua non* in its constitution: thence foreign Courts have a certainty, that nothing can be done by common counsel in this nation. If one of those Ministers officially takes up a business with spirit, it serves only the better to signalise the meanness of the rest, and the discord of them all. His colleagues in office are in haste to shake him off, and to disclaim the whole of his proceedings. Of this nature was that astonishing transaction, in which Lord Rochford, our Ambassador at Paris, remonstrated against the attempt upon Corsica, in consequence of a direct authority from Lord Shelburne. This remonstrance the French Minister treated with the contempt that was natural; as he was assured, from the Ambassador of his Court to ours, that these orders of Lord Shelburne were not supported by the rest of the (I had like to have said British) Administration. Lord Rochford, a man of spirit, could not endure this situation. The consequences were, however, curious. He returns from Paris, and comes home full of anger. Lord Shelburne, who gave the orders, is obliged to give up the seals. Lord Rochford, who obeyed these orders, receives them. He goes, however, into another department of the same office, that he might not be obliged officially to acquiesce in one situation, under what he had officially remonstrated against in another. At Paris, the Duke of Choiseul considered this office arrangement as a compliment to him: here it was spoke of as an attention to the delicacy of Lord Rochford. But whether the compliment was to one or both, to this nation it was the same. By this transaction the condition of our Court lay exposed in all its nakedness. Our office correspondence has lost all pretence to authenticity; British policy is brought into derision in those nations, that a while ago trembled at the power of our arms, whilst they looked up with confidence to the equity, firmness, and candour, which shone in all our negotiations. I represent this matter exactly in the light in which it has been universally received.

\* \* \* \* \*

Such has been the aspect of our foreign politics under the influence of a *double Cabinet*. With such an arrangement at Court, it is impossible it should have been otherwise. Nor is it possible that this scheme should have a better effect upon the government of our dependencies, the first, the dearest, and most delicate objects of the interior policy of this empire. The Colonies know that Administration is separated from the Court, divided within itself, and detested by the nation. The double Cabinet has, in both the parts of it, shown the most malignant dispositions towards them, without being able to do them the smallest mischief.

They are convinced, by sufficient experience, that no plan, either of lenity or rigour, can be pursued with uniformity and perseverance. Therefore they turn their eyes entirely from Great Britain, where they have neither dependence on friendship nor apprehension from enmity. They look to themselves, and their own arrangements. They grow every day into alienation from this country; and whilst they are becoming disconnected with our Government, we have not the consolation to find that they are even friendly in their new independence. Nothing can equal the futility, the weakness, the rashness, the timidity, the perpetual contradiction, in the management of our affairs in that part of the world. A volume might be written on this melancholy subject; but it were better to leave it entirely to the reflections of the reader himself, than not to treat it in the extent it deserves.

In what manner our domestic economy is affected by this system, it is needless to explain. It is the perpetual subject of their own complaints.

The Court party resolve the whole into faction. Having said something before upon this subject, I shall only observe here, that, when they give this account of the prevalence of faction, they present no very favourable aspect of the confidence of the people in their own Government. They may be assured, that however they amuse themselves with a variety of projects for substituting something else in the place of that great and only foundation of Government, the confidence of the people, every attempt will but make their condition worse. When men imagine that their food is only a cover for poison, and when they neither love nor trust the hand that serves it, it is not the name of the roast beef of Old England that will persuade them to sit down to the table that is spread for them. When the people conceive that laws, and tribunals, and even popular assemblies, are perverted from the ends of their institution, they find in those names of degenerated establishments only new motives to discontent. Those bodies, which, when full of life and beauty, lay in their arms and were their joy and comfort; when dead and putrid, become but the more loathsome from remembrance of former endearments. A sullen gloom, and furious disorder, prevail by fits: the nation loses its relish for peace and prosperity, as it did in that season of fulness which opened our troubles in the time of Charles the First. A species of men to whom a state of order would become a sentence of obscurity, are nourished into a dangerous magnitude by the heat of intestine disturbances; and it is no wonder that, by a sort of sinister piety, they cherish, in their turn, the disorders which are the parents of all their consequence. Superficial observers consider such persons as the cause of the public uneasiness, when, in truth, they are nothing more than the effect of it. Good men look upon this distracted scene with sorrow and indignation. Their hands are tied behind them. They are despoiled of all the power which might enable them to reconcile the strength of Government with the rights of the people. They stand in a most distressing alternative. But in the election among evils they hope better things from temporary confusion, than from established servitude. In the mean time, the voice of law is not to be heard. Fierce licentiousness begets violent restraints. The military arm is the sole reliance; and then, call your constitution what you please, it is the sword that governs. The civil power, like every other that calls in the aid of an ally stronger than itself, perishes by the assistance it receives. But the contrivers of this scheme of Government will not trust solely to the military power, because they are cunning men. Their restless and crooked spirit drives them to rake in the dirt of every kind of expedient. Unable to rule the multitude, they endeavour to raise divisions amongst them. One mob is hired to destroy another; a procedure which at once encourages the boldness of the populace, and justly increases their discontent. Men become pensioners of state on account of their abilities in the array of riot, and the discipline of confusion. Government is put under the disgraceful necessity of protecting from the severity of the laws that very licentiousness, which the laws had been before violated to repress. Everything partakes of the original disorder. Anarchy predominates without freedom, and servitude without submission or subordination. These are the consequences inevitable to our public peace, from the scheme of rendering the executory Government at once odious and feeble; of freeing Administration from the constitutional and salutary control of Parliament, and inventing for it a new control, unknown to the constitution, an *interior* Cabinet; which brings the whole body of Government into confusion and contempt.

* * * * *

After having stated, as shortly as I am able, the effects of this system on our foreign affairs, on the policy of our Government with regard to our dependencies, and on the interior economy of the Commonwealth; there remains only, in this part of my design, to say something of the grand principle which first recommended this system at Court. The pretence was to prevent the King from being enslaved by a faction, and made a prisoner in his closet. This scheme might have been expected to answer at least its own end, and to indemnify the King, in his personal capacity, for all the confusion into which it has thrown his Government. But has it in reality answered this purpose? I am sure, if it had, every affectionate subject would have one motive for enduring with patience all the evils which attend it.

In order to come at the truth in this matter, it may not be amiss to consider it somewhat in detail. I speak here of the King, and not of the Crown; the interests of which we have already touched. Independent of that greatness which a King possesses merely by being a representative of the national dignity, the things in which he may have an individual interest seem to be these: wealth accumulated; wealth spent in magnificence, pleasure, or beneficence; personal respect and attention; and above all, private ease and repose of mind. These compose the inventory of prosperous circumstances, whether they regard a Prince or a subject; their enjoyments differing only in the scale upon which they are formed.

Suppose then we were to ask, whether the King has been richer than his predecessors in accumulated wealth, since the establishment of the plan of

Favouritism? I believe it will be found that the picture of royal indigence which our Court has presented until this year, has been truly humiliating. Nor has it been relieved from this unseemly distress, but by means which have hazarded the affection of the people, and shaken their confidence in Parliament. If the public treasures had been exhausted in magnificence and splendour, this distress would have been accounted for, and in some measure justified. Nothing would be more unworthy of this nation, than with a mean and mechanical rule, to mete out the splendour of the Crown. Indeed, I have found very few persons disposed to so ungenerous a procedure. But the generality of people, it must be confessed, do feel a good deal mortified, when they compare the wants of the Court with its expenses. They do not behold the cause of this distress in any part of the apparatus of Royal magnificence. In all this, they see nothing but the operations of parsimony, attended with all the consequences of profusion. Nothing expended, nothing saved. Their wonder is increased by their knowledge, that besides the revenue settled on his Majesty's Civil List to the amount of £800,000 a year, he has a farther aid, from a large pension list, near £90,000 a year, in Ireland; from the produce of the Duchy of Lancaster (which we are told has been greatly improved); from the revenue of the Duchy of Cornwall; from the American quit-rents; from the four and a half per cent. duty in the Leeward Islands; this last worth to be sure considerably more than £40,000 a year. The whole is certainly not much short of a million annually.

These are revenues within the knowledge and cognizance of our national Councils. We have no direct right to examine into the receipts from his Majesty's German Dominions, and the Bishopric of Osnaburg. This is unquestionably true. But that which is not within the province of Parliament, is yet within the sphere of every man's own reflection. If a foreign Prince resided amongst us, the state of his revenues could not fail of becoming the subject of our speculation. Filled with an anxious concern for whatever regards the welfare of our Sovereign, it is impossible, in considering the miserable circumstances into which he has been brought, that this obvious topic should be entirely passed over. There is an opinion universal, that these revenues produce something not inconsiderable, clear of all charges and establishments. This produce the people do not believe to be hoarded, nor perceive to be spent. It is accounted for in the only manner it can, by supposing that it is drawn away, for the support of that Court faction, which, whilst it distresses the nation, impoverishes the Prince in every one of his resources. I once more caution the reader, that I do not urge this consideration concerning the foreign revenue, as if I supposed we had a direct right to examine into the expenditure of any part of it; but solely for the purpose of showing how little this system of Favouritism has been advantageous to the Monarch himself; which, without magnificence, has sunk him into a state of unnatural poverty; at the same time that he possessed every means of affluence, from ample revenues, both in this country and in other parts of his dominions.

Has this system provided better for the treatment becoming his high and sacred character, and secured the King from those disgusts attached to the necessity of employing men who are not personally agreeable? This is a topic upon which for many reasons I could wish to be silent; but the pretence of securing against such causes of uneasiness, is the corner-stone of the Court party. It has however so happened, that if I were to fix upon any one point, in which this system has been more particularly and shamefully blameable, the effects which it has produced would justify me in choosing for that point its tendency to degrade the personal dignity of the Sovereign, and to expose him to a thousand contradictions and mortifications. It is but too evident in what manner these projectors of Royal greatness have fulfilled all their magnificent promises. Without recapitulating all the circumstances of the reign, every one of which is more or less a melancholy proof of the truth of what I have advanced, let us consider the language of the Court but a few years ago, concerning most of the persons now in the external Administration: let me ask, whether any enemy to the personal feelings of the Sovereign, could possibly contrive a keener instrument of mortification, and degradation of all dignity, than almost every part and member of the present arrangement? Nor, in the whole course of our history, has any compliance with the will of the people ever been known to extort from any Prince a greater contradiction to all his own declared affections and dislikes, than that which is now adopted, in direct opposition to every thing the people approve and desire.

An opinion prevails, that greatness has been more than once advised to submit to certain condescensions towards individuals, which have been denied to the entreaties of a nation. For the meanest and most dependent instrument of this system knows, that there are hours when its existence may depend upon his adherence to it; and he takes his advantage accordingly. Indeed it is a law of nature, that whoever is necessary to what we have made our object, is sure, in some way, or in some time or other, to become our master. All this however is submitted to, in order to avoid that monstrous evil of governing in concurrence with the opinion of the people. For it seems to be laid down as a maxim, that a King has some sort of interest in giving uneasiness to his subjects: that all who are pleasing to them, are to be of course disagreeable to him: that as soon as the persons who are odious at Court are known to be odious to the people, it is snatched at as a lucky occasion of showering down upon them all kinds of emoluments and honours. None are considered as well-wishers to the Crown, but those who advised to some unpopular course of action; none capable of serving it, but those who are obliged to call at every instant upon all its power for the safety of their lives. None are supposed to be fit priests in the temple of Government, but the persons who are compelled to fly into it for sanctuary. Such is the effect of this refined project; such is ever the result of all the contrivances which are used to free men from the servitude of their reason, and from the necessity of ordering their affairs according to their evident interests. These contrivances oblige them to run into a real and ruinous servitude, in order to avoid a supposed restraint that might be attended with advantage.

If therefore this system has so ill answered its own grand pretence of saving the King from the necessity of employing persons disagreeable to him, has it given more peace and tranquillity to his Majesty's private hours? No, most certainly. The father of his people cannot possibly enjoy repose, while his family is in such a state of distraction. Then what has the Crown or the King profited by all this fine-wrought scheme? Is he more rich, or more splendid, or more powerful, or more at his ease, by so many labours and contrivances? Have they not beggared his Exchequer, tarnished the splendour of his Court, sunk his dignity, galled his feelings, discomposed the whole order and happiness of his private life?

It will be very hard, I believe, to state in what respect the King has profited by that faction which presumptuously choose to call themselves *his friends*.

If particular men had grown into an attachment, by the distinguished honour of the society of their Sovereign, and, by being the partakers of his amusements, came sometimes to prefer the gratification of his personal inclinations to the support of his high character, the thing would be very natural, and it would be excusable enough. But the pleasant part of the story is, that these *King's friends* have no more ground for usurping such a title, than a resident freeholder in Cumberland or in Cornwall. They are only known to their Sovereign by kissing his hand, for the offices, pensions, and grants into which they have deceived his benignity. May no storm ever come, which will put the firmness of their attachment to the proof; and which, in the midst of confusions and terrors, and sufferings, may demonstrate the eternal difference between a true and severe friend to the Monarchy, and a slippery sycophant of the Court; *Quantum infido scurræ distabit amicus!*

* * * * *

So far I have considered the effect of the Court system, chiefly as it operates upon the executive Government, on the temper of the people and on the happiness of the Sovereign. It remains that we should consider, with a little attention, its operation upon Parliament.

Parliament was indeed the great object of all these politics, the end at which they aimed, as well as the instrument by which they were to operate. But, before Parliament could be made subservient to a system, by which it was to be degraded from the dignity of a national council, into a mere member of the Court, it must be greatly changed from its original character.

In speaking of this body, I have my eye chiefly on the House of Commons. I hope I shall be indulged in a few observations on the nature and character of that assembly; not with regard to its *legal form and power*, but to its *spirit*, and to the purposes it is meant to answer in the constitution.

The House of Commons was supposed originally to be *no part of the standing Government of this country*. It was considered as a control, issuing immediately from the people, and speedily to be resolved into the mass from whence it arose. In this respect it was in the higher part of Government what juries are in the lower. The capacity of a magistrate being transitory, and that of a citizen permanent, the latter capacity it was hoped would of course preponderate in all discussions, not only between the people and the standing authority of the Crown, but between the people and the fleeting authority of the House of Commons itself. It was hoped that, being of a middle nature between subject and Government, they would feel with a more tender and a nearer interest everything that concerned the people, than the other remoter and more permanent parts of Legislature.

Whatever alterations time and the necessary accommodation of business may have introduced, this character can never be sustained, unless the House of Commons shall be made to bear some stamp of the actual disposition of the people at large. It would (among public misfortunes) be an evil more natural and tolerable, that the House of Commons should be infected with every epidemical frenzy of the people, as this would indicate some consanguinity, some sympathy of nature with their constituents, than that they should in all cases be wholly untouched by the opinions and feelings of the people out of doors. By this want of sympathy they would cease to be a House of Commons. For it is not the derivation of the power of that House from the people, which makes it in a distinct sense their representative. The King is the representative of the people; so are the Lords; so are the Judges. They all are trustees for the people, as well as the Commons; because no power is given for the sole sake of the holder; and although Government certainly is an institution of Divine authority, yet its forms, and the persons who administer it, all originate from the people.

A popular origin cannot therefore be the characteristical distinction of a popular representative. This belongs equally to all parts of Government, and in all forms. The virtue, spirit, and essence of a House of Commons consists in its being the express image of the feelings of the nation. It was not instituted to be a control upon the people, as of late it has been taught, by a doctrine of the most pernicious tendency. It was designed as a control *for* the people. Other institutions have been formed for the purpose of checking popular excesses; and they are, I apprehend, fully adequate to their object. If not, they ought to be made so. The House of Commons, as it was never intended for the support of peace and subordination, is miserably appointed for that service; having no stronger weapon than its Mace, and no better officer than its Serjeant-at-Arms, which it can command of its own proper authority. A vigilant and jealous eye over executory and judicial magistracy; an anxious care of public money, an openness, approaching towards facility, to public complaint; these seem to be the true characteristics of a House of Commons. But an addressing House of Commons, and a petitioning nation; a House of Commons full of confidence, when the nation is plunged in despair; in the utmost harmony with Ministers, whom the people regard with the utmost abhorrence; who vote thanks, when the public opinion calls upon them for impeachments; who are eager to grant, when the general voice demands account; who, in all disputes between the people and Administration, presume against the people; who punish their disorder, but refuse even to inquire into the provocations to them; this is an unnatural, a monstrous state of things in this constitution. Such an Assembly may be a great, wise, awful senate; but it is not, to any popular purpose, a House of Commons. This change from an immediate state of procuration and delegation to a course of acting as from original power, is the way in which all the popular magistracies in the world have been perverted from their purposes. It is indeed their greatest and sometimes their incurable corruption. For there is a material distinction between that corruption by which particular points are carried against reason (this is a thing which cannot be prevented by human wisdom, and is of less consequence), and the corruption of the principle itself. For then the evil is not accidental, but settled. The distemper becomes the natural habit.

For my part, I shall be compelled to conclude the principle of Parliament to be totally corrupted, and therefore its ends entirely defeated, when I see two symptoms: first, a rule of indiscriminate support to all Ministers; because this destroys the very end of Parliament as a control, and is a general previous sanction to misgovernment; and secondly, the setting up any claims adverse to the right of free election; for this tends to subvert the legal authority by which the House of Commons sits.

I know that, since the Revolution, along with many dangerous, many useful powers of Government have been weakened. It is absolutely necessary to have frequent recourse to the Legislature. Parliaments must therefore sit every year, and for great part of the year. The dreadful disorders of frequent elections have also necessitated a septennial instead of a triennial duration. These circumstances, I mean the constant habit of authority, and the infrequency of elections, have tended very much to draw the House of Commons towards the character of a standing Senate. It is a disorder which has arisen from the cure of greater disorders; it has arisen from the extreme difficulty of reconciling liberty under a monarchical Government, with external strength and with internal tranquillity.

It is very clear that we cannot free ourselves entirely from this great inconvenience; but I would not increase an evil, because I was not able to remove it; and because it was not in my power to keep the House of Commons religiously true to its first principles, I would not argue for carrying it to a total oblivion of them. This has been the great scheme of power in our time. They who will not conform their conduct to the public good, and cannot support it by the prerogative of the Crown, have adopted a new plan. They have totally abandoned the shattered and old-fashioned fortress of prerogative, and made a lodgment in the stronghold of Parliament itself. If they have any evil design to which there is no ordinary legal power commensurate, they bring it into Parliament. In Parliament the whole is executed from the beginning to the end. In Parliament the power of obtaining their object is absolute, and the safety in the proceeding perfect: no rules to confine, no after reckonings to terrify. Parliament cannot with any great propriety punish others for things in which they themselves have been accomplices. Thus the control of Parliament upon the executory power is lost; because Parliament is made to partake in every considerable act of Government. *Impeachment, that great guardian of the purity of the Constitution, is in danger of being lost, even to the idea of it.*

By this plan several important ends are answered to the Cabal. If the authority of Parliament supports itself, the credit of every act of Government, which they contrive, is saved; but if the act be so very odious that the whole strength of Parliament is insufficient to recommend it, then Parliament is itself discredited; and this discredit increases more and more that indifference to the constitution, which it is the constant aim of its enemies, by their abuse of Parliamentary powers, to render general among the people. Whenever Parliament is persuaded to assume the offices of executive Government, it will lose all the confidence, love, and veneration which it has ever enjoyed, whilst it was supposed the *corrective* and *control* of the acting powers of the State. This would be the event, though its conduct in such a perversion of its functions should be tolerably just and moderate; but if it should be iniquitous, violent, full of passion, and full of faction, it would be considered as the most intolerable of all the modes of tyranny.

For a considerable time this separation of the representatives from their constituents went on with a silent progress; and had those, who conducted the plan for their total separation, been persons of temper and abilities any way equal to the magnitude of their design, the success would have been infallible; but by their precipitancy they have laid it open in all its nakedness; the nation is alarmed at it; and the event may not be pleasant to the contrivers of the scheme. In the last session, the corps called the *King's friends* made a hardy attempt all at once, *to alter the right of election itself*; to put it into the power of the House of Commons to disable any person disagreeable to them from sitting in Parliament, without any other rule than their own pleasure; to make incapacities, either general for descriptions of men, or particular for individuals; and to take into their body, persons who avowedly had never been chosen by the majority of legal electors, nor agreeably to any known rule of law.

The arguments upon which this claim was founded and combated, are not my business here. Never has a subject been more amply and more learnedly handled, nor upon one side, in my opinion, more satisfactorily; they who are not convinced by what is already written would not receive conviction *though one arose from the dead.*

I too have thought on this subject; but my purpose here, is only to consider it as a part of the favourite project of Government; to observe on the motives which led to it; and to trace its political consequences.

A violent rage for the punishment of Mr. Wilkes was the pretence of the whole. This gentleman, by setting himself strongly in opposition to the Court Cabal, had become at once an object of their persecution, and of the popular favour. The hatred of the Court party pursuing, and the countenance of the people protecting him, it very soon became not at all a question on the man, but a trial of strength between the two parties. The advantage of the victory in this particular contest was the present, but not the only, nor by any means, the principal, object. Its operation upon the character of the House of Commons was the great point in view. The point to be gained by the Cabal was this: that a precedent should be established, tending to show, *That the favour of the people was not so sure a road as the favour of the Court even to popular honours and popular trusts.* A strenuous resistance to every appearance of lawless power; a spirit of independence carried to some degree of enthusiasm; an inquisitive character to discover, and a bold one to display, every corruption and every error of Government; these are the qualities which recommend a man to a seat in the House of Commons, in open and merely popular elections. An indolent and submissive disposition; a disposition to think charitably of all the actions of men in power, and to live in a mutual intercourse of favours with them; an inclination rather to countenance a strong use of authority, than to bear any sort of licentiousness on the part of the people; these are unfavourable qualities in an open election for Members of Parliament.

The instinct which carries the people towards the choice of the former, is justified by reason; because a man of such a character, even in its exorbitancies, does not directly contradict the purposes of a trust, the end of which is a control on power. The latter character, even when it is not in its extreme, will execute this trust but very imperfectly; and, if deviating to the least excess, will certainly frustrate instead of forwarding the purposes of a control on Government. But when the House of Commons was to be new modelled, this principle was not only to be changed, but reversed. Whilst any errors committed in support of power were left to the law, with every advantage of favourable construction, of mitigation, and finally of pardon; all excesses on the side of liberty, or in pursuit of popular favour, or in defence of popular rights and privileges, were not only to be punished by the rigour of the known law, but by a *discretionary* proceeding, which brought on *the loss of the popular object itself*. Popularity was to be rendered, if not directly penal, at least highly dangerous. The favour of the people might lead even to a disqualification of representing them. Their odium might become, strained through the medium of two or three constructions, the means of sitting as the trustee of all that was dear to them. This is punishing the offence in the offending part. Until this time, the opinion of the people, through the power of an Assembly, still in some sort popular, led to the greatest honours and emoluments in the gift of the Crown. Now the principle is reversed; and the favour of the Court is the only sure way of obtaining and holding those honours which ought to be in the disposal of the people.

It signifies very little how this matter may be quibbled away. Example, the only argument of effect in civil life, demonstrates the truth of my proposition. Nothing can alter my opinion concerning the pernicious tendency of this example, until I see some man for his indiscretion in the support of power, for his violent and intemperate servility, rendered incapable of sitting in parliament. For as it now stands, the fault of overstraining popular qualities, and, irregularly if you please, asserting popular privileges, has led to disqualification; the opposite fault never has produced the slightest punishment. Resistance to power has shut the door of the House of Commons to one man; obsequiousness and servility, to none.

Not that I would encourage popular disorder, or any disorder. But I would leave such offences to the law, to be punished in measure and proportion. The laws of this country are for the most part constituted, and wisely so, for the general ends of Government, rather than for the preservation of our particular liberties. Whatever therefore is done in support of liberty, by persons not in public trust, or not acting merely in that trust, is liable to be more or less out of the ordinary course of the law; and the law itself is sufficient to animadvert upon it with great severity. Nothing indeed can hinder that severe letter from crushing us, except the temperaments it may receive from a trial by jury. But if the habit prevails of *going beyond the law*, and superseding this judicature, of carrying offences, real or supposed, into the legislative bodies, who shall establish themselves into *courts of criminal equity*, (so *the Star Chamber* has been called by Lord Bacon,) all the evils of the *Star* Chamber are revived. A large and liberal construction in ascertaining offences, and a discretionary power in punishing them, is the idea of criminal equity; which is in truth a monster in Jurisprudence. It signifies nothing whether a court for this purpose be a Committee of Council, or a House of Commons, or a House of Lords; the liberty of the subject will be equally subverted by it. The true end and purpose of that House of Parliament which entertains such a jurisdiction will be destroyed by it.

I will not believe, what no other man living believes, that Mr. Wilkes was punished for the indecency of his publications, or the impiety of his ransacked closet. If he had fallen in a common slaughter of libellers and blasphemers, I could well believe that nothing more was meant than was pretended. But when I see, that, for years together, full as impious, and perhaps more dangerous writings to religion, and virtue, and order, have not been punished, nor their authors discountenanced; that the most audacious libels on Royal Majesty have passed without notice; that the most treasonable invectives against the laws, liberties, and constitution of the country, have not met with the slightest animadversion; I must consider this as a shocking and shameless pretence. Never did an envenomed scurrility against everything sacred and civil, public and private, rage through the kingdom with such a furious and unbridled licence. All this while the peace of the nation must be shaken, to ruin one libeller, and to tear from the populace a single favourite.

Nor is it that vice merely skulks in an obscure and contemptible impunity. Does not the public behold with indignation, persons not only generally scandalous in their lives, but the identical persons who, by their society, their instruction, their example, their encouragement, have drawn this man into the very faults which have furnished the Cabal with a pretence for his persecution, loaded with every kind of favour, honour, and distinction, which a Court can bestow? Add but the crime of servility (the *foedum crimem servitutis*) to every other crime, and the whole mass is immediately transmuted into virtue, and becomes the just subject of reward and honour. When therefore I reflect upon this method pursued by the Cabal in distributing rewards and punishments, I must conclude that Mr. Wilkes is the object of persecution, not on account of what he has done in common with others who are the objects of reward, but for that in which he differs from many of them: that he is pursued for the spirited dispositions which are blended with his vices; for his unconquerable firmness, for his resolute, indefatigable, strenuous resistance against oppression.

In this case, therefore, it was not the man that was to be punished, nor his faults that were to be discountenanced. Opposition to acts of power was to be marked by a kind of civil proscription. The popularity which should arise from such an opposition was to be shown unable to protect it. The qualities by which court is made to the people, were to render every fault inexpiable, and every error irretrievable. The qualities by which court is made to power, were to cover and to sanctify everything. He that will have a sure and honourable seat, in the House of Commons, must take care how he adventures to cultivate popular qualities; otherwise he may, remember the old maxim, *Breves et infaustos populi Romani amores.* If, therefore, a pursuit of popularity expose a man to greater dangers than a disposition to servility, the principle which is the life and soul of popular elections will perish out of the Constitution.

It behoves the people of England to consider how the House of Commons under the operation of these examples must of necessity be constituted. On the side of the Court will be, all honours, offices, emoluments; every sort of personal gratification to avarice or vanity; and, what is of more moment to most gentlemen, the means of growing, by innumerable petty services to individuals, into a spreading interest in their country. On the other hand, let us suppose a person unconnected with the Court, and in opposition to its system. For his own person, no office, or emolument, or title; no promotion ecclesiastical, or civil, or military, or naval, for children, or brothers, or kindred. In vain an expiring interest in a borough calls for offices, or small livings, for the children of mayors, and aldermen, and capital burgesses. His court rival has them all. He can do an infinite number of acts of generosity and kindness, and even of public spirit. He can procure indemnity from quarters. He can procure advantages in trade. He can get pardons for offences. He can obtain a thousand favours, and avert a thousand evils. He may, while he betrays every valuable interest of the kingdom, be a benefactor, a patron, a father, a guardian angel, to his borough. The unfortunate independent member has nothing to offer, but harsh refusal, or pitiful excuse, or despondent representation of a hopeless interest. Except from his private fortune, in which he may be equalled, perhaps exceeded, by his Court competitor, he has no way of showing any one good quality, or of making a single friend. In the House, he votes for ever in a dispirited minority. If he speaks, the doors are locked. A body of loquacious placemen go out to tell the world, that all he aims at, is to get into office. If he has not the talent of elocution, which is the case of many as wise and knowing men as any in the House, he is liable to all these inconveniences, without the eclat which attends upon any tolerably successful exertion of eloquence. Can we conceive a more discouraging post of duty than this? Strip it of the poor reward of popularity; suffer even the excesses committed in defence of the popular interest to become a ground for the majority of that House to form a disqualification out of the line of the law, and at their pleasure, attended not only with the loss of the franchise, but with every kind of personal disgrace; if this shall happen, the people of this kingdom may be assured that they cannot be firmly or faithfully served by any man. It is out of the nature of men and things that they should; and their presumption will be equal to their folly, if they expect it. The power of the people, within the laws, must show itself sufficient to protect every representative in the animated performance of his duty, or that duty cannot be performed. The House of Commons can never be a control on other parts of Government, unless they are controlled themselves by their constituents; and unless these constituents possess some right in the choice of that House, which it is not in the power of that House to take away. If they suffer this power of arbitrary incapacitation to stand, they have utterly perverted every other power of the House of Commons. The late proceeding, I will not say, *is* contrary to law; it *must* be so; for the power which is claimed cannot, by any possibility, be a legal power in any limited member of Government.

The power which they claim, of declaring incapacities, would not be above the just claims of a final judicature, if they had not laid it down as a leading principle, that they had no rule in the exercise of this claim but their own *discretion*. Not one of their abettors has ever undertaken to assign the principle of unfitness, the species or degree of delinquency, on which the House of Commons will expel, nor the mode of proceeding upon it, nor the evidence upon which it is established. The direct consequence of which is, that the first franchise of an Englishman, and that on which all the rest vitally depend, is to be forfeited for some offence which no man knows, and which is to be proved by no known rule whatsoever of legal evidence. This is so anomalous to our whole constitution, that I will venture to say, the most trivial right, which the subject claims, never was, nor can be, forfeited in such a manner.

The whole of their usurpation is established upon this method of arguing. We do not make laws. No; we do not contend for this power. We only declare law; and, as we are a tribunal both competent and supreme, what we declare to be law becomes law, although it should not have been so before. Thus the circumstance of having no appeal from their jurisdiction is made to imply that they have no rule in the exercise of it: the judgment does not derive its validity from its conformity to the law; but preposterously the law is made to attend on the judgment; and the rule of the judgment is no other than the *occasional will of the House.* An arbitrary discretion leads, legality follows; which is just the very nature and description of a legislative act.

This claim in their hands was no barren theory. It was pursued into its utmost consequences; and a dangerous principle has begot a correspondent practice. A systematic spirit has been shown upon both sides. The electors of Middlesex chose a person whom the House of Commons had voted incapable; and the House of Commons has taken in a member whom the electors of Middlesex had not chosen. By a construction on that legislative power which had been assumed, they declared that the true legal sense of the country was contained in the minority, on that occasion; and might, on a resistance to a vote of incapacity, be contained in any minority.

When any construction of law goes against the spirit of the privilege it was meant to support, it is a vicious construction. It is material to us to be represented really and bona fide, and not in forms, in types, and shadows, and fictions of law. The right of election was not established merely as a *matter of form,* to satisfy some method and rule of technical reasoning; it was not a principle which might substitute a *Titius* or a *Maevius,* a *John Doe* or *Richard Roe,* in the place of a man specially chosen; not a principle which was just as well satisfied with one man as with another. It is a right, the effect of which is to give to the people that man, and that man only, whom by their voices, actually, not constructively given, they declare that they know, esteem, love, and trust. This right is a matter within their own power of judging and feeling; not an *ens rationis* and creature of law: nor can those devices, by which anything else is substituted in the place of such an actual choice, answer in the least degree the end of representation.

I know that the courts of law have made as strained constructions in other cases. Such is the construction in common recoveries. The method of construction which in that case gives to the persons in remainder, for their security and representative, the door-keeper, crier, or sweeper of the Court, or some other shadowy being without substance or effect, is a fiction of a very coarse texture. This was however suffered, by the acquiescence of the whole kingdom, for ages; because the evasion of the old Statute of Westminster, which authorised perpetuities, had more sense and utility than the law which was evaded. But an attempt to turn the right of election into such a farce and mockery as a fictitious fine and recovery, will, I hope, have another fate; because the laws which give it are infinitely dear to us, and the evasion is infinitely contemptible.

The people indeed have been told, that this power of discretionary disqualification is vested in hands that they may trust, and who will be sure not to abuse it to their prejudice. Until I find something in this argument differing from that on which every mode of despotism has been defended, I shall not be inclined to pay it any great compliment. The people are satisfied to trust themselves with the exercise of their own privileges, and do not desire this kind intervention of the House of Commons to free them from the burthen. They are certainly in the right. They ought not to trust the House of Commons with a power over their franchises; because the constitution, which placed two other co-ordinate powers to control it, reposed no such confidence in that body. It were a folly well deserving servitude for its punishment, to be full of confidence where the laws are full of distrust; and to give to an House of Commons, arrogating to its sole resolution the most harsh and odious part of legislative authority, that degree of submission which is due only to the Legislature itself.

When the House of Commons, in an endeavour to obtain new advantages at the expense of the other orders of the State, for the benefits of the *Commons at large*, have pursued strong measures; if it were not just, it was at least natural, that the constituents should connive at all their proceedings; because we were ourselves ultimately to profit. But when this submission is urged to us, in a contest between the representatives and ourselves, and where nothing can be put into their scale which is not taken from ours, they fancy us to be children when they tell us they are our representatives, our own flesh and blood, and that all the stripes they give us are for our good. The very desire of that body to have such a trust contrary to law reposed in them, shows that they are not worthy of it. They certainly will abuse it; because all men possessed of an uncontrolled discretionary power leading to the aggrandisement and profit of their own body have always abused it: and I see no particular sanctity in our times, that is at all likely, by a miraculous operation, to overrule the course of nature.

But we must purposely shut our eyes, if we consider this matter merely as a contest between the House of Commons and the Electors. The true contest is between the Electors of the Kingdom and the Crown; the Crown acting by an instrumental House of Commons. It is precisely the same, whether the Ministers of the Crown can disqualify by a dependent House of Commons, or by a dependent court of *Star Chamber*, or by a dependent court of King's Bench. If once Members of Parliament can be practically convinced that they do not depend on the affection or opinion of the people for their political being, they will give themselves over, without even an appearance of reserve, to the influence of the Court.

Indeed, a Parliament unconnected with the people, is essential to a Ministry unconnected with the people; and therefore those who saw through what mighty difficulties the interior Ministry waded, and the exterior were dragged, in this business, will conceive of what prodigious importance, the new corps of *King's men* held this principle of occasional and personal incapacitation, to the whole body of their design.

When the House of Commons was thus made to consider itself as the master of its constituents, there wanted but one thing to secure that House against all possible future deviation towards popularity; an unlimited fund of money to be laid out according to the pleasure of the Court.

\* \* \* \* \*

To complete the scheme of bringing our Court to a resemblance to the neighbouring Monarchies, it was necessary, in effect, to destroy those appropriations of revenue, which seem to limit the property, as the other laws had done the powers, of the Crown. An opportunity for this purpose was taken, upon an application to Parliament for payment of the debts of the Civil List; which in 1769 had amounted to £513,000. Such application had been made upon former occasions; but to do it in the former manner would by no means answer the present purpose.

Whenever the Crown had come to the Commons to desire a supply for the discharging of debts due on the Civil List, it was always asked and granted with one of the three following qualifications; sometimes with all of them. Either it was stated that the revenue had been diverted from its purposes by Parliament; or that those duties had fallen short of the sum for which they were given by Parliament, and that the intention of the Legislature had not been fulfilled; or that the money required to discharge the Civil List debt was to be raised chargeable on the Civil List duties. In the reign of Queen Anne, the Crown was found in debt. The lessening and granting away some part of her revenue by Parliament was alleged as the cause of that debt, and pleaded as an equitable ground (such it certainly was), for discharging it. It does not appear that the duties which wore then applied to the ordinary Government produced clear above £580,000 a year; because, when they were afterwards granted to George the First, £120,000 was added, to complete the whole to £700,000 a year. Indeed it was then asserted, and, I have no doubt, truly, that for many years the nett produce did not amount to above £550,000. The Queen's extraordinary charges were besides very considerable; equal, at least, to any we have known in our time. The application to Parliament was not for an absolute grant of money, but to empower the Queen to raise it by borrowing upon the Civil List funds.

The Civil List debt was twice paid in the reign of George the First. The money was granted upon the same plan which had been followed in the reign of Queen Anne. The Civil List revenues were then mortgaged for the sum to be raised, and stood charged with the ransom of their own deliverance.

George the Second received an addition to his Civil List. Duties were granted for the purpose of raising £800,000 a year. It was not until he had reigned nineteen years, and after the last rebellion, that he called upon Parliament for a discharge of the Civil List debt. The extraordinary charges brought on by the rebellion, account fully for the necessities of the Crown. However, the extraordinary charges of Government were not thought a ground fit to be relied on. A deficiency of the Civil List duties for several years before was stated as the principal, if not the sole, ground on which an application to Parliament could be justified. About this time the produce of these duties had fallen pretty low; and even upon an average of the whole reign they never produced £800,000 a year clear to the Treasury.

That Prince reigned fourteen years afterwards: not only no new demands were made, but with so much good order were his revenues and expenses regulated, that, although many parts of the establishment of the Court were upon a larger and more liberal scale than they have been since, there was a considerable sum in hand, on his decease, amounting to about £170,000, applicable to the service of the Civil List of his present Majesty. So that, if this reign commenced with a greater charge than usual, there was enough, and more than enough, abundantly to supply all the extraordinary expense. That the Civil List should have been exceeded in the two former reigns, especially in the reign of George the First, was not at all surprising. His revenue was but £700,000 annually; if it ever produced so much clear. The prodigious and dangerous disaffection to the very being of the establishment, and the cause of a Pretender then powerfully abetted from abroad, produced many demands of an extraordinary nature both abroad and at home. Much management and great expenses were necessary. But the throne of no Prince has stood upon more unshaken foundations than that of his present Majesty.

To have exceeded the sum given for the Civil List, and to have incurred a debt without special authority of Parliament, was, *prima facie*, a criminal act: as such Ministers ought naturally rather to have withdrawn it from the inspection, than to have exposed it to the scrutiny, of Parliament. Certainly they ought, of themselves, officially to have come armed with every sort of argument, which, by explaining, could excuse a matter in itself of presumptive guilt. But the terrors of the House of Commons are no longer for Ministers.

On the other hand, the peculiar character of the House of Commons, as trustee of the public purse, would have led them to call with a punctilious solicitude for every public account, and to have examined into them with the most rigorous accuracy.

The capital use of an account is, that the reality of the charge, the reason of incurring it, and the justice and necessity of discharging it, should all appear antecedent to the payment. No man ever pays first, and calls for his account afterwards; because he would thereby let out of his hands the principal, and indeed only effectual, means of compelling a full and fair one. But, in national business, there is an additional reason for a previous production of every account. It is a cheek, perhaps the only one, upon a corrupt and prodigal use of public money. An account after payment is to no rational purpose an account. However, the House of Commons thought all these to be antiquated principles; they were of opinion that the most Parliamentary way of proceeding was, to pay first what the Court thought proper to demand, and to take its chance for an examination into accounts at some time of greater leisure.

The nation had settled £800,000 a year on the Crown, as sufficient for the purpose of its dignity, upon the estimate of its own Ministers. When Ministers came to Parliament, and said that this allowance had not been sufficient for the purpose, and that they had incurred a debt of £500,000, would it not have been natural for Parliament first to have asked, how, and by what means, their appropriated allowance came to be insufficient? Would it not have savoured of some attention to justice, to have seen in what periods of Administration this debt had been originally incurred; that they might discover, and if need were, animadvert on the persons who were found the most culpable? To put their hands upon such articles of expenditure as they thought improper or excessive, and to secure, in future, against such misapplication or exceeding? Accounts for any other purposes are but a matter of curiosity, and no genuine Parliamentary object. All the accounts which could answer any Parliamentary end were refused, or postponed by previous questions. Every idea of prevention was rejected, as conveying an improper suspicion of the Ministers of the Crown.

When every leading account had been refused, many others were granted with sufficient facility.

But with great candour also, the House was informed, that hardly any of them could be ready until the next session; some of them perhaps not so soon. But, in order firmly to establish the precedent of *payment previous to account*, and to form it into a settled rule of the House, the god in the machine was brought down, nothing less than the wonder-working *Law of Parliament*. It was alleged, that it is the law of Parliament, when any demand comes from the Crown, that the House must go immediately into the Committee of Supply; in which Committee it was allowed, that the production and examination of accounts would be quite proper and regular. It was therefore carried that they should go into the Committee without delay, and without accounts, in order to examine with great order and regularity things that could not possibly come before them. After this stroke of orderly and Parliamentary wit and humour, they went into the Committee, and very generously voted the payment.

There was a circumstance in that debate too remarkable to be overlooked. This debt of the Civil List was all along argued upon the same footing as a debt of the State, contracted upon national authority. Its payment was urged as equally pressing upon the public faith and honour; and when the whole year's account was stated, in what is called *The Budget*, the Ministry valued themselves on the payment of so much public debt, just as if they had discharged £500,000 of navy or exchequer bills. Though, in truth, their payment, from the Sinking Fund, of debt which was never contracted by Parliamentary authority, was, to all intents and purposes, so much debt incurred. But such is the present notion of public credit and payment of debt. No wonder that it produces such effects.

Nor was the House at all more attentive to a provident security against future, than it had been to a vindictive retrospect to past, mismanagements. I should have thought indeed that a Ministerial promise, during their own continuance in office, might have been given, though this would have been but a poor security for the public. Mr. Pelham gave such an assurance, and he kept his word. But nothing was capable of extorting from our Ministers anything which had the least resemblance to a promise of confining the expenses of the Civil List within the limits which had been settled by Parliament. This reserve of theirs I look upon to be equivalent to the clearest declaration that they were resolved upon a contrary course.

However, to put the matter beyond all doubt, in the Speech from the Throne, after thanking Parliament for the relief so liberally granted, the Ministers inform the two Houses that they will *endeavour* to confine the expenses of the Civil Government—within what limits, think you? those which the law had prescribed? Not in the least—"such limits as the *honour of the Crown* can possibly admit."

Thus they established an arbitrary standard for that dignity which Parliament had defined and limited to a legal standard. They gave themselves, under the lax and indeterminate idea of the *honour of the Crown*, a full loose for all manner of dissipation, and all manner of corruption. This arbitrary standard they were not afraid to hold out to both Houses; while an idle and inoperative Act of Parliament, estimating the dignity of the Crown at £800,000, and confining it to that sum, adds to the number of obsolete statutes which load the shelves of libraries without any sort of advantage to the people.

After this proceeding, I suppose that no man can be so weak as to think that the Crown is limited to any settled allowance whatsoever. For if the Ministry has £800,000 a year by the law of the land, and if by the law of Parliament all the debts which exceed it are to be paid previous to the production of any account, I presume that this is equivalent to an income with no other limits than the abilities of the subject and the moderation of the Court—that is to say, it is such in income as is possessed by every absolute Monarch in Europe. It amounts, as a person of great ability said in the debate, to an unlimited power of drawing upon the Sinking Fund. Its effect on the public credit of this kingdom must be obvious; for in vain is the Sinking Fund the great buttress of all the rest, if it be in the power of the Ministry to resort to it for the payment of any debts which they may choose to incur, under the name of the Civil List, and through the medium of a committee, which thinks itself obliged by law to vote supplies without any other account than that of the more existence of the debt.

Five hundred thousand pounds is a serious sum. But it is nothing to the prolific principle upon which the sum was voted—a principle that may be well called, *the fruitful mother of a hundred more*. Neither is the damage to public credit of very great consequence when compared with that which results to public morals and to the safety of the Constitution, from the exhaustless mine of corruption opened by the precedent, and to be wrought by the principle of the late payment of the debts of the Civil List. The power of discretionary disqualification by one law of Parliament, and the necessity of paying every debt of the Civil List by another law of Parliament, if suffered to pass unnoticed, must establish such a fund of rewards and terrors as will make Parliament the best appendage and support of arbitrary power that ever was invented by the wit of man. This is felt. The quarrel is begun between the Representatives and the People. The Court Faction have at length committed them.

In such a strait the wisest may well be perplexed, and the boldest staggered. The circumstances are in a great measure new. We have hardly any landmarks from the wisdom of our ancestors to guide us. At best we can only follow the spirit of their proceeding in other cases. I know the diligence with which my observations on our public disorders have been made. I am very sure of the integrity of the motives on which they are published: I cannot be equally confident in any plan for the absolute cure of those disorders, or for their certain future prevention. My aim is to bring this matter into more public discussion. Let the sagacity of others work upon it. It is not uncommon for medical writers to describe histories of diseases, very accurately, on whose cure they can say but very little.

The first ideas which generally suggest themselves for the cure of Parliamentary disorders are, to shorten the duration of Parliaments, and to disqualify all, or a great number of placemen, from a seat in the House of Commons. Whatever efficacy there may be in those remedies, I am sure in the present state of things it is impossible to apply them. A restoration of the right of free election is a preliminary indispensable to every other reformation. What alterations ought afterwards to be made in the constitution is a matter of deep and difficult research.

If I wrote merely to please the popular palate, it would indeed be as little troublesome to me as to another to extol these remedies, so famous in speculation, but to which their greatest admirers have never attempted seriously to resort in practice. I confess them, that I have no sort of reliance upon either a Triennial Parliament or a Place-bill. With regard to the former, perhaps, it might rather serve to counteract than to promote the ends that are proposed by it. To say nothing of the horrible disorders among the people attending frequent elections, I should be fearful of committing, every three years, the independent gentlemen of the country into a contest with the Treasury. It is easy to see which of the contending parties would be ruined first. Whoever has taken a careful view of public proceedings, so as to endeavour to ground his speculations on his experience, must have observed how prodigiously greater the power of Ministry is in the first and last session of a Parliament, than it is in the intermediate periods, when Members sit a little on their seats. The persons of the greatest Parliamentary experience, with whom I have conversed, did constantly, in canvassing the fate of questions, allow something to the Court side, upon account of the elections depending or imminent. The evil complained of, if it exists in the present state of things, would hardly be removed by a triennial Parliament: for, unless the influence of Government in elections can be entirely taken away, the more frequently they return, the more they will harass private independence; the more generally men will be compelled to fly to the settled systematic interest of Government, and to the resources of a boundless Civil List. Certainly something may be done, and ought to be done, towards lessening that influence in elections; and this will be necessary upon a plan either of longer or shorter duration of Parliament. But nothing can so perfectly remove the evil, as not to render such contentions, foot frequently repeated, utterly ruinous, first to independence of fortune, and then to independence of spirit. As I am only giving an opinion on this point, and not at all debating it in an adverse line, I hope I may be excused in another observation. With great truth I may aver that I never remember to have talked on this subject with any man much conversant with public business who considered short Parliaments as a real improvement of the Constitution. Gentlemen, warm in a popular cause, are ready enough to attribute all the declarations of such persons to corrupt motives. But the habit of affairs, if, on one hand, it tends to corrupt the mind, furnishes it, on the other, with the, means of better information. The authority of such persons will always have some weight. It may stand upon a par with the speculations of those who are less practised in business; and who, with perhaps purer intentions, have not so effectual means of judging. It is besides an effect of vulgar and puerile malignity to imagine that every Statesman is of course corrupt: and that his opinion, upon every constitutional point, is solely formed upon some sinister interest.

The next favourite remedy is a Place-bill. The same principle guides in both: I mean the opinion which is entertained by many of the infallibility of laws and regulations, in the cure of public distempers. Without being as unreasonably doubtful as many are unwisely confident, I will only say, that this also is a matter very well worthy of serious and mature reflection. It is not easy to foresee what the effect would be of disconnecting with Parliament, the greatest part of those who hold civil employments, and of such mighty and important bodies as the military and naval establishments. It were better, perhaps, that they should have a corrupt interest in the forms of the constitution, than they should have none at all. This is a question altogether different from the disqualification of a particular description of Revenue Officers from seats in Parliament; or, perhaps, of all the lower sorts of them from votes in elections. In the former case, only the few are affected; in the latter, only the inconsiderable. But a great official, a great professional, a great military and naval interest, all necessarily comprehending many people of the first weight, ability, wealth, and spirit, has been gradually formed in the kingdom. These new interests must be let into a share of representation, else possibly they may be inclined to destroy those institutions of which they are not permitted to partake. This is not a thing to be trifled with: nor is it every well-meaning man that is fit to put his hands to it. Many other serious considerations occur. I do not open them here, because they are not directly to my purpose; proposing only to give the reader some taste of the difficulties that attend all capital changes in the Constitution; just to hint the uncertainty, to say no worse, of being able to prevent the Court, as long as it has the means of influence abundantly in its power, from applying that influence to Parliament; and perhaps, if the public method were precluded, of doing it in some worse and more dangerous method. Underhand and oblique ways would be studied. The science of evasion, already tolerably understood, would then be brought to the greatest perfection. It is no inconsiderable part of wisdom, to know how much of an evil ought to be tolerated; lest, by attempting a degree of purity impracticable in degenerate times and manners, instead of cutting off the subsisting ill practices, new corruptions might be produced for the concealment and security of the old. It were better, undoubtedly, that no influence at all could affect the mind of a Member of Parliament. But of all modes of influence, in my opinion, a place under the Government is the least disgraceful to the man who holds it, and by far the most safe to the country. I would not shut out that sort of influence which is open and visible, which is connected with the dignity and the service of the State, when it is not in my power to prevent the influence of contracts, of subscriptions, of direct bribery, and those innumerable methods of clandestine corruption, which are abundantly in the hands of the Court, and which will be applied as long as these means of corruption, and the disposition to be corrupted, have existence amongst us. Our Constitution stands on a nice equipoise, with steep precipices and deep waters upon all sides of it. In removing it from a dangerous leaning towards one side, there may be a risk of oversetting it on the other. Every project of a material change in a Government so complicated as ours, combined at the same time with external circumstances still more complicated, is a matter full of difficulties; in which a considerate man will not be too ready to decide; a prudent man too ready to undertake; or an honest man too ready to promise. They do not respect the public nor themselves, who engage for more than they are sure that they ought to attempt, or that they are able to perform. These are my sentiments, weak perhaps, but honest and unbiassed; and submitted entirely to the opinion of grave men, well affected to the constitution of their country, and of experience in what may best promote or hurt it.

Indeed, in the situation in which we stand, with an immense revenue, an enormous debt, mighty establishments, Government itself a great banker and a great merchant, I see no other way for the preservation of a decent attention to public interest in the Representatives, but *the interposition of the body of the people itself*, whenever it shall appear, by some flagrant and notorious act, by some capital innovation, that these Representatives are going to over-leap the fences of the law, and to introduce an arbitrary power. This interposition is a most unpleasant remedy. But, if it be a legal remedy, it is intended on some occasion to be used; to be used then only, when it is evident that nothing else can hold the Constitution to its true principles.

* * * * *

The distempers of Monarchy were the great subjects of apprehension and redress, in the last century; in this, the distempers of Parliament. It is not in Parliament alone that the remedy for Parliamentary disorders can be completed; hardly, indeed, can it begin there. Until a confidence in Government is re-established, the people ought to be excited to a more strict and detailed attention to the conduct of their Representatives. Standards, for judging more systematically upon their conduct, ought to be settled in the meetings of counties and corporations. Frequent and correct lists of the voters in all important questions ought to be procured.

By such means something may be done. By such means it may appear who those are, that, by an indiscriminate support of all Administrations, have totally banished all integrity and confidence out of public proceedings; have confounded the best men with the worst; and weakened and dissolved, instead of strengthening and compacting, the general frame of Government. If any person is more concerned for government and order than for the liberties of his country, even he is equally concerned to put an end to this course of indiscriminate support. It is this blind and undistinguishing support that feeds the spring of those very disorders, by which he is frighted into the arms of the faction which contains in itself the source of all disorders, by enfeebling all the visible and regular authority of the State. The distemper is increased by his injudicious and preposterous endeavours, or pretences, for the cure of it.

An exterior Administration, chosen for its impotency, or after it is chosen purposely rendered impotent, in order to be rendered subservient, will not be obeyed. The laws themselves will not be respected, when those who execute them are despised: and they will be despised, when their power is not immediate from the Crown, or natural in the kingdom. Never were Ministers better supported in Parliament. Parliamentary support comes and goes with office, totally regardless of the man, or the merit. Is Government strengthened? It grows weaker and weaker. The popular torrent gains upon it every hour. Let us learn from our experience. It is not support that is wanting to Government, but reformation. When Ministry rests upon public opinion, it is not indeed built upon a rock of adamant; it has, however, some stability. But when it stands upon private humour, its structure is of stubble, and its foundation is on quicksand. I repeat it again—He that supports every Administration, subverts all Government. The reason is this. The whole business in which a Court usually takes an interest goes on at present equally well, in whatever hands, whether high or low, wise or foolish, scandalous or reputable; there is nothing, therefore, to hold it firm to any one body of men, or to any one consistent scheme of politics. Nothing interposes to prevent the full operation of all the caprices and all the passions of a Court upon the servants of the public. The system of Administration is open to continual shocks and changes, upon the principles of the meanest cabal, and the most contemptible intrigue. Nothing can be solid and permanent. All good men at length fly with horror from such a service. Men of rank and ability, with the spirit which ought to animate such men in a free state, while they decline the jurisdiction of dark cabal on their actions and their fortunes, will, for both, cheerfully put themselves upon their country. They will trust an inquisitive and distinguishing Parliament; because it does inquire, and does distinguish. If they act well, they know that, in such a Parliament, they will be supported against any intrigue; if they act ill, they know that no intrigue can protect them. This situation, however awful, is honourable. But in one hour, and in the self-same Assembly, without any assigned or assignable cause, to be precipitated from the highest authority to the most marked neglect, possibly into the greatest peril of life and reputation, is a situation full of danger, and destitute of honour. It will be shunned equally by every man of prudence, and every man of spirit.

Such are the consequences of the division of Court from the Administration; and of the division of public men among themselves. By the former of these, lawful Government is undone; by the latter, all opposition to lawless power is rendered impotent. Government may in a great measure be restored, if any considerable bodies of men have honesty and resolution enough never to accept Administration, unless this garrison of *King's* meat, which is stationed, as in a citadel, to control and enslave it, be entirely broken and disbanded, and every work they have thrown up be levelled with the ground. The disposition of public men to keep this corps together, and to act under it, or to co-operate with it, is a touchstone by which every Administration ought in future to be tried. There has not been one which has not sufficiently experienced the utter incompatibility of that faction with the public peace, and with all the ends of good Government; since, if they opposed it, they soon lost every power of serving the Crown; if they submitted to it they lost all the esteem of their country. Until Ministers give to the public a full proof of their entire alienation from that system, however plausible their pretences, we may be sure they are more intent on the emoluments than the duties of office. If they refuse to give this proof, we know of what stuff they are made. In this particular, it ought to be the electors' business to look to their Representatives. The electors ought to esteem it no less culpable in their Member to give a single vote in Parliament to such an Administration, than to take an office under it; to endure it, than to act in it. The notorious infidelity and versatility of Members of Parliament, in their opinions of men and things, ought in a particular manner to be considered by the electors in the inquiry which is recommended to them. This is one of the principal holdings of that destructive system which has endeavoured to unhinge all the virtuous, honourable, and useful connections in the kingdom.

This cabal has, with great success, propagated a doctrine which serves for a colour to those acts of treachery; and whilst it receives any degree of countenance, it will be utterly senseless to look for a vigorous opposition to the Court Party. The doctrine is this: That all political connections are in their nature factious, and as such ought to be dissipated and destroyed; and that the rule for forming Administrations is mere personal ability, rated by the judgment of this cabal upon it, and taken by drafts from every division and denomination of public men. This decree was solemnly promulgated by the head of the Court corps, the Earl of Bute himself, in a speech which he made, in the year 1766, against the then Administration, the only Administration which, he has ever been known directly and publicly to oppose.

It is indeed in no way wonderful, that such persons should make such declarations. That connection and faction are equivalent terms, is an opinion which has been carefully inculcated at all times by unconstitutional Statesmen. The reason is evident. Whilst men are linked together, they easily and speedily communicate the alarm of an evil design. They are enabled to fathom it with common counsel, and to oppose it with united strength. Whereas, when they lie dispersed, without concert, order, or discipline, communication is uncertain, counsel difficult, and resistance impracticable. Where men are not acquainted with each other's principles, nor experienced in each other's talents, nor at all practised in their mutual habitudes and dispositions by joint efforts in business; no personal confidence, no friendship, no common interest, subsisting among them; it is evidently impossible that they can act a public part with uniformity, perseverance, or efficacy. In a connection, the most inconsiderable man, by adding to the weight of the whole, has his value, and his use; out of it, the greatest talents are wholly unserviceable to the public. No man, who is not inflamed by vainglory into enthusiasm, can flatter himself that his single, unsupported, desultory, unsystematic endeavours, are of power to defeat, the subtle designs and united cabals of ambitious citizens. When bad men combine, the good must associate; else they will fall, one by one, an unpitied sacrifice in a contemptible struggle.

It is not enough in a situation of trust in the commonwealth, that a man means well to his country; it is not enough that in his single person he never did an evil act, but always voted according to his conscience, and even harangued against every design which he apprehended to be prejudicial to the interests of his country. This innoxious and ineffectual character, that seems formed upon a plan of apology and disculpation, falls miserably short of the mark of public duty. That duty demands and requires, that what is right should not only be made known, but made prevalent; that what is evil should not only be detected, but defeated. When the public man omits to put himself in a situation of doing his duty with effect, it is an omission that frustrates the purposes of his trust almost as much as if he had formally betrayed it. It is surely no very rational account of a man's life that he has always acted right; but has taken special care to act in such a manner that his endeavours could not possibly be productive of any consequence.

I do not wonder that the behaviour of many parties should have made persons of tender and scrupulous virtue somewhat out of humour with all sorts of connection in politics. I admit that people frequently acquire in such confederacies a narrow, bigoted, and proscriptive spirit; that they are apt to sink the idea of the general good in this circumscribed and partial interest. But, where duty renders a critical situation a necessary one, it is our business to keep free from the evils attendant upon it, and not to fly from the situation itself. If a fortress is seated in an unwholesome air, an officer of the garrison is obliged to be attentive to his health, but he must not desert his station. Every profession, not excepting the glorious one of a soldier, or the sacred one of a priest, is liable to its own particular vices; which, however, form no argument against those ways of life; nor are the vices themselves inevitable to every individual in those professions. Of such a nature are connections in politics; essentially necessary for the full performance of our public duty, accidentally liable to degenerate into faction. Commonwealths are made of families, free Commonwealths of parties also; and we may as well affirm, that our natural regards and ties of blood tend inevitably to make men bad citizens, as that the bonds of our party weaken those by which we are held to our country.

Some legislators went so far as to make neutrality in party a crime against the State. I do not know whether this might not have been rather to overstrain the principle. Certain it is, the best patriots in the greatest commonwealths have always commanded and promoted such connections. *Idem sentire de republica*, was with them a principal ground of friendship and attachment; nor do I know any other capable of forming firmer, dearer, more pleasing, more honourable, and more virtuous habitudes. The Romans carried this principle a great way. Even the holding of offices together, the disposition of which arose from chance, not selection, gave rise to a relation which continued for life. It was called *necessitudo sortis*; and it was looked upon with a sacred reverence. Breaches of any of these kinds of civil relation were considered as acts of the most distinguished turpitude. The whole people was distributed into political societies, in which they acted in support of such interests in the State as they severally affected. For it was then thought no crime, to endeavour by every honest means to advance to superiority and power those of your own sentiments and opinions. This wise people was far from imagining that those connections had no tie, and obliged to no duty; but that men might quit them without shame, upon every call of interest. They believed private honour to be the great foundation of public trust; that friendship was no mean step towards patriotism; that he who, in the common intercourse of life, showed he regarded somebody besides himself, when he came to act in a public situation, might probably consult some other interest than his own. Never may we become *plus sages que les sages*, as the French comedian has happily expressed it—wiser than all the wise and good men who have lived before us. It was their wish, to see public and private virtues, not dissonant and jarring, and mutually destructive, but harmoniously combined, growing out of one another in a noble and orderly gradation, reciprocally supporting and supported. In one of the most fortunate periods of our history this country was governed by a connection; I mean the great connection of Whigs in the reign of Queen Anne. They were complimented upon the principle of this connection by a poet who was in high esteem with them. Addison, who knew their sentiments, could not praise them for what they considered as no proper subject of commendation. As a poet who knew his business, he could not applaud them for a thing which in general estimation was not highly reputable. Addressing himself to Britain,

> "Thy favourites grow not up by fortune's sport,
> Or from the crimes or follies of a Court;
> On the firm basis of desert they rise,
> From long-tried faith, and friendship's holy ties."

The Whigs of those days believed that the only proper method of rising into power was through bard essays of practised friendship and experimented fidelity. At that time it was not imagined that patriotism was a bloody idol, which required the sacrifice of children and parents, or dearest connections in private life, and of all the virtues that rise from those relations. They were not of that ingenious paradoxical morality to imagine that a spirit of moderation was properly shown in patiently bearing the sufferings of your friends, or that disinterestedness was clearly manifested at the expense of other people's fortune. They believed that no men could act with effect who did not act in concert; that no men could act in concert who did not act with confidence; that no men could act with confidence who were not bound together by common opinions, common affections, and common interests.

These wise men, for such I must call Lord Sunderland, Lord Godolphin, Lord Somers, and Lord Marlborough, were too well principled in these maxims, upon which the whole fabric of public strength is built, to be blown off their ground by the breath of every childish talker. They were not afraid that they should be called an ambitious Junto, or that their resolution to stand or fall together should, by placemen, be interpreted into a scuffle for places.

Party is a body of men united for promoting by their joint endeavours the national interest, upon some particular principle in which they are all agreed. For my part, I find it impossible to conceive that any one believes in his own politics, or thinks them to be of any weight, who refuses to adopt the means of having them reduced into practice. It is the business of the speculative philosopher to mark the proper ends of Government. It is the business of the politician, who is the philosopher in action, to find out proper means towards those ends, and to employ them with effect. Therefore, every honourable connection will avow it as their first purpose to pursue every just method to put the men who hold their opinions into such a condition as may enable them to carry their common plans into execution, with all the power and authority of the State. As this power is attached to certain situations, it is their duty to contend for these situations. Without a proscription of others, they are bound to give to their own party the preference in all things, and by no means, for private considerations, to accept any offers of power in which the whole body is not included, nor to suffer themselves to be led, or to be controlled, or to be over-balanced, in office or in council, by those who contradict, the very fundamental principles on which their party is formed, and even those upon which every fair connection must stand. Such a generous contention for power, on such manly and honourable maxims, will easily be distinguished from the mean and interested struggle for place and emolument. The very style of such persons will serve to discriminate them from those numberless impostors who have deluded the ignorant with professions incompatible with human practice, and have afterwards incensed them by practices below the level of vulgar rectitude.

It is an advantage to all narrow wisdom and narrow morals that their maxims have a plausible air, and, on a cursory view, appear equal to first principles. They are light and portable. They are as current as copper coin, and about as valuable. They serve equally the first capacities and the lowest, and they are, at least, as useful to the worst men as the best. Of this stamp is the cant of *Not men, but measures*; a sort of charm, by which many people got loose from every honourable engagement. When I see a man acting this desultory and disconnected part, with as much detriment to his own fortune as prejudice to the cause of any party, I am not persuaded that he is right, but I am ready to believe he is in earnest. I respect virtue in all its situations, even when it is found in the unsuitable company of weakness. I lament to see qualities, rare and valuable, squandered away without any public utility. But when a gentleman with great visible emoluments abandons the party in which he has long acted, and tells you it is because he proceeds upon his own judgment that he acts on the merits of the several measures as they arise, and that he is obliged to follow his own conscience, and not that of others, he gives reasons which it is impossible to controvert, and discovers a character which it is impossible to mistake. What shall we think of him who never differed from a certain set of men until the moment they lost their power, and who never agreed with them in a single instance afterwards? Would not such a coincidence of interest and opinion be rather fortunate? Would it not be an extraordinary cast upon the dice that a man's connections should degenerate into faction, precisely at the critical moment when they lose their power or he accepts a place? When people desert their connections, the desertion is a manifest fact, upon which a direct simple issue lies, triable by plain men. Whether a *measure* of Government be right or wrong is *no matter of fact*, but a mere affair of opinion, on which men may, as they do, dispute and wrangle without end. But whether the individual thinks the measure right or wrong is a point at still a greater distance from the reach of all human decision. It is therefore very convenient to politicians not to put the judgment of their conduct on overt acts, cognisable in any ordinary court, but upon such a matter as can be triable only in that secret tribunal, where they are sure of being heard with favour, or where at worst the sentence will be only private whipping.

I believe the reader would wish to find no substance in a doctrine which has a tendency to destroy all test of character as deduced from conduct. He will therefore excuse my adding something more towards the further clearing up a point which the great convenience of obscurity to dishonesty has been able to cover with some degree of darkness and doubt.

In order to throw an odium on political connection, these politicians suppose it a necessary incident to it that you are blindly to follow the opinions of your party when in direct opposition to your own clear ideas, a degree of servitude that no worthy man could bear the thought of submitting to, and such as, I believe, no connections (except some Court factions) ever could be so senselessly tyrannical as to impose. Men thinking freely will, in particular instances, think differently. But still, as the greater Part of the measures which arise in the course of public business are related to, or dependent on, some great leading general principles in Government, a man must be peculiarly unfortunate in the choice of his political company if he does not agree with them at least nine times in ten. If he does not concur in these general principles upon which the party is founded, and which necessarily draw on a concurrence in their application, he ought from the beginning to have chosen some other, more conformable to his opinions. When the question is in its nature doubtful, or not very material, the modesty which becomes an individual, and (in spite of our Court moralists) that partiality which becomes a well-chosen friendship, will frequently bring on an acquiescence in the general sentiment. Thus the disagreement will naturally be rare; it will be only enough to indulge freedom, without violating concord or disturbing arrangement. And this is all that ever was required for a character of the greatest uniformity and steadiness in connection. How men can proceed without any connection at all is to me utterly incomprehensible. Of what sort of materials must that man be made, how must he be tempered and put together, who can sit whole years in Parliament, with five hundred and fifty of his fellow-citizens, amidst the storm of such tempestuous passions, in the sharp conflict of so many wits, and tempers, and characters, in the agitation of such mighty questions, in the discussion of such vast and ponderous interests, without seeing any one sort of men, whose character, conduct, or disposition would lead him to associate himself with them, to aid and be aided, in any one system of public utility?

I remember an old scholastic aphorism, which says that "the man who lives wholly detached from others must be either an angel or a devil." When I see in any of these detached gentlemen of our times the angelic purity, power, and beneficence, I shall admit them to be angels. In the meantime, we are born only to be men. We shall do enough if we form ourselves to be good ones. It is therefore our business carefully to cultivate in our minds, to rear to the most perfect vigour and maturity, every sort of generous and honest feeling that belongs to our nature. To bring the, dispositions that are lovely in private life into the service and conduct of the commonwealth; so to be patriots, as not to forget we are gentlemen. To cultivate friendships, and to incur enmities. To have both strong, but both selected: in the one, to be placable; in the other, immovable. To model our principles to our duties and our situation. To be fully persuaded that all virtue which is impracticable is spurious, and rather to run the risk of falling into faults in a course which leads us to act with effect and energy than to loiter out our days without blame and without use. Public life is a situation of power and energy; he trespasses against his duty who sleeps upon his watch, as well as he that goes over to the enemy.

There is, however, a time for all things. It is not every conjuncture which calls with equal force upon the activity of honest men; but critical exigences now and then arise, and I am mistaken if this be not one of them. Men will see the necessity of honest combination, but they may see it when it is too late. They may embody when it will be ruinous to themselves, and of no advantage to the country; when, for want of such a timely union as may enable them to oppose in favour of the laws, with the laws on their side, they may at length find themselves under the necessity of conspiring, instead of consulting. The law, for which they stand, may become a weapon in the hands of its bitterest enemies; and they will be cast, at length, into that miserable alternative, between slavery and civil confusion, which no good man can look upon without horror, an alternative in which it is impossible he should take either part with a conscience perfectly at repose. To keep that situation of guilt and remorse at the utmost distance is, therefore, our first obligation. Early activity may prevent late and fruitless violence. As yet we work in the light. The scheme of the enemies of public tranquillity has disarranged, it has not destroyed us.

If the reader believes that there really exists such a Faction as I have described, a Faction ruling by the private inclinations of a Court, against the general sense of the people; and that this Faction, whilst it pursues a scheme for undermining all the foundations of our freedom, weakens (for the present at least) all the powers of executory Government, rendering us abroad contemptible, and at home distracted; he will believe, also, that nothing but a firm combination of public men against this body, and that, too, supported by the hearty concurrence of the people at large, can possibly get the better of it. The people will see the necessity of restoring public men to an attention to the public opinion, and of restoring the Constitution to its original principles. Above all, they will endeavour to keep the House of Commons from assuming a character which does not belong to it. They will endeavour to keep that House, for its existence for its powers, and its privileges, as independent of every other, and as dependent upon themselves, as possible. This servitude is to a House of Commons (like obedience to the Divine law), "perfect freedom." For if they once quit this natural, rational, and liberal obedience, having deserted the only proper foundation of their power, they must seek a support in an abject and unnatural dependence somewhere else. When, through the medium of this just connection with their constituents, the genuine dignity of the House of Commons is restored, it will begin to think of casting from it, with scorn, as badges of servility, all the false ornaments of illegal power, with which it has been, for some time, disgraced. It will begin to think of its old office of CONTROL. It will not suffer that last of evils to predominate in the country; men without popular confidence, public opinion, natural connection, or natural trust, invested with all the powers of Government.

When they have learned this lesson themselves, they will be willing and able to teach the Court, that it is the true interest of the Prince to have but one Administration; and that one composed of those who recommend themselves to their Sovereign through the opinion of their country, and not by their obsequiousness to a favourite. Such men will serve their Sovereign with affection and fidelity; because his choice of them, upon such principles, is a compliment to their virtue. They will be able to serve him effectually; because they will add the weight of the country to the force of the executory power. They will be able to serve their King with dignity; because they will never abuse his name to the gratification of their private spleen or avarice. This, with allowances for human frailty, may probably be the general character of a Ministry, which thinks itself accountable to the House of Commons, when the House of Commons thinks itself accountable to its constituents. If other ideas should prevail, things must remain in their present confusion, until they are hurried into all the rage of civil violence; or until they sink into the dead repose of despotism.

# SPEECH ON THE MIDDLESEX ELECTION
## FEBRUARY, 1771

Mr. Speaker,—In every complicated Constitution (and every free Constitution is complicated) cases will arise, when the several orders of the State will clash with one another, and disputes will arise about the limits of their several rights and privileges. It may be almost impossible to reconcile them.

Carry the principle on by which you expelled Mr. Wilkes, there is not a man in the House, hardly a man in the nation, who may not be disqualified. That this House should have no power of expulsion is a hard saying. That this House should have a general discretionary power of disqualification is a dangerous saying. That the people should not choose their own representative, is a saying that shakes the Constitution. That this House should name the representative, is a saying which, followed by practice, subverts the constitution. They have the right of electing, you have a right of expelling; they of choosing, you of judging, and only of judging, of the choice. What bounds shall be set to the freedom of that choice? Their right is prior to ours, we all originate there. They are the mortal enemies of the House of Commons, who would persuade them to think or to act as if they were a self-originated magistracy, independent of the people and unconnected with their opinions and feelings. Under a pretence of exalting the dignity, they undermine the very foundations of this House. When the question is asked here, what disturbs the people, whence all this clamour, we apply to the treasury-bench, and they tell us it is from the efforts of libellers and the wickedness of the people, a worn-out ministerial pretence. If abroad the people are deceived by popular, within we are deluded by ministerial, cant. The question amounts to this, whether you mean to be a legal tribunal, or an arbitrary and despotic assembly. I see and I feel the delicacy and difficulty of the ground upon which we stand in this question. I could wish, indeed, that they who advised the Crown had not left Parliament in this very ungraceful distress, in which they can neither retract with dignity nor persist with justice. Another parliament might have satisfied the people without lowering themselves. But our situation is not in our own choice: our conduct in that situation is all that is in our own option. The substance of the question is, to put bounds to your own power by the rules and principles of law. This is, I am sensible, a difficult thing to the corrupt, grasping, and ambitious part of human nature. But the very difficulty argues and enforces the necessity of it. First, because the greater the power, the more dangerous the abuse. Since the Revolution, at least, the power of the nation has all flowed with a full tide into the House of Commons. Secondly, because the House of Commons, as it is the most powerful, is the most corruptible part of the whole Constitution. Our public wounds cannot be concealed; to be cured, they must be laid open. The public does think we are a corrupt body. In our legislative capacity we are, in most instances, esteemed a very wise body. In our judicial, we have no credit, no character at, all. Our judgments stink in the nostrils of the people. They think us to be not only without virtue, but without shame. Therefore, the greatness of our power, and the great and just opinion of our corruptibility and our corruption, render it necessary to fix some bound, to plant some landmark, which we are never to exceed. That is what the bill proposes. First, on this head, I lay it down as a fundamental rule in the law and constitution of this country, that this House has not by itself alone a legislative authority in any case whatsoever. I know that the contrary was the doctrine of the usurping House of Commons which threw down the fences and bulwarks of law, which annihilated first the lords, then the Crown, then its constituents. But the first thing that was done on the restoration of the Constitution was to settle this point. Secondly, I lay it down as a rule, that the power of occasional incapacitation, on discretionary grounds, is a legislative power. In order to establish this principle, if it should not be sufficiently proved by being stated, tell me what are the criteria, the characteristics, by which you distinguish between a legislative and a juridical act. It will be necessary to state, shortly, the difference between a legislative and a juridical act. A legislative act has no reference to any rule but these two: original justice, and discretionary application. Therefore, it can give rights; rights where no rights existed before; and it can take away rights where they were before established. For the law, which binds all others, does not and cannot bind the law-maker; he, and he alone, is above the law. But a judge, a person exercising a judicial capacity, is neither to apply to original justice, nor to a discretionary application of it. He goes to justice and discretion only at second hand, and through the medium of some superiors. He is to work neither upon his opinion of the one nor of the other; but upon a fixed rule, of which he has not the making, but singly and solely the application to the case.

The power assumed by the House neither is, nor can be, judicial power exercised according to known law. The properties of law are, first, that it should be known; secondly, that it should be fixed and not occasional. First, this power cannot be according to the first property of law; because no man does or can know it, nor do you yourselves know upon what grounds you will vote the incapacity of any man. No man in Westminster Hall, or in any court upon earth, will say that is law, upon which, if a man going to his counsel should say to him, "What is my tenure in law of this estate?" he would answer, "Truly, sir, I know not; the court has no rule but its own discretion: they will determine." It is not a, fixed law, because you profess you vary it according to the occasion, exercise it according to your discretion; no man can call for it as a right. It is argued that the incapacity is not originally voted, but a consequence of a power of expulsion: but if you expel, not upon legal, but upon arbitrary, that is, upon discretionary grounds, and the incapacity is *ex vi termini* and inclusively comprehended in the expulsion, is not the incapacity voted in the expulsion? Are they not convertible terms? and, if incapacity is voted to be inherent in expulsion, if expulsion be arbitrary, incapacity is arbitrary also. I have, therefore, shown that the power of incapacitation is a legislative power; I have shown that legislative power does not belong to the House of Commons; and, therefore, it follows that the House of Commons has not a power of incapacitation.

I know not the origin of the House of Commons, but am very sure that it did not create itself; the electors wore prior to the elected; whose rights originated either from the people at large, or from some other form of legislature, which never could intend for the chosen a power of superseding the choosers.

If you have not a power of declaring an incapacity simply by the mere act of declaring it, it is evident to the most ordinary reason you cannot have a right of expulsion, inferring, or rather, including, an incapacity, For as the law, when it gives any direct right, gives also as necessary incidents all the means of acquiring the possession of that right, so where it does not give a right directly, it refuses all the means by which such a right may by any mediums be exercised, or in effect be indirectly acquired. Else it is very obvious that the intention of the law in refusing that right might be entirely frustrated, and the whole power of the legislature baffled. If there be no certain invariable rule of eligibility, it were better to get simplicity, if certainty is not to be had; and to resolve all the franchises of the subject into this one short proposition—the will and pleasure of the House of Commons.

The argument, drawn from the courts of law, applying the principles of law to new cases as they emerge, is altogether frivolous, inapplicable, and arises from a total ignorance of the bounds between civil and criminal jurisdiction, and of the separate maxims that govern these two provinces of law, that are eternally separate. Undoubtedly the courts of law, where a new case comes before them, as they do every hour, then, that there may be no defect in justice, call in similar principles, and the example of the nearest determination, and do everything to draw the law to as near a conformity to general equity and right reason as they can bring it with its being a fixed principle. *Boni judicis est ampliare justitiam*—that is, to make open and liberal justice. But in criminal matters this parity of reason, and these analogies, ever have been, and ever ought to be, shunned.

Whatever is incident to a court of judicature, is necessary to the House of Commons, as judging in elections. But a power of making incapacities is not necessary to a court of judicature; therefore a power of making incapacities is not necessary to the House of Commons.

Incapacity, declared by whatever authority, stands upon two principles: first, an incapacity arising from the supposed incongruity of two duties in the commonwealth; secondly, an incapacity arising from unfitness by infirmity of nature, or the criminality of conduct. As to the first class of incapacities, they have no hardship annexed to them. The persons so incapacitated are paid by one dignity for what they abandon in another, and, for the most part, the situation arises from their own choice. But as to the second, arising from an unfitness not fixed by nature, but superinduced by some positive acts, or arising from honourable motives, such as an occasional personal disability, of all things it ought to be defined by the fixed rule of law—what Lord Coke calls the Golden Metwand of the Law, and not by the crooked cord of discretion. Whatever is general is better born. We take our common lot with men of the same description. But to be selected and marked out by a particular brand of unworthiness among our fellow-citizens, is a lot of all others the hardest to be borne: and consequently is of all others that act which ought only to be trusted to the legislature, as not only legislative in its nature, but of all parts of legislature the most odious. The question is over, if this is shown not to be a legislative act. But what is very usual and natural, is to corrupt judicature into legislature. On this point it is proper to inquire whether a court of judicature, which decides without appeal, has it as a necessary incident of such judicature, that whatever it decides *de jure* is law. Nobody will, I hope, assert this, because the direct consequence would be the entire extinction of the difference between true and false judgments. For, if the judgment makes the law, and not the law directs the judgment, it is impossible there could be such a thing as an illegal judgment given.

But, instead of standing upon this ground, they introduce another question, wholly foreign to it, whether it ought not to be submitted to as if it were law. And then the question is, By the Constitution of this country, what degree of submission is due to the authoritative acts of a limited power? This question of submission, determine it how you please, has nothing to do in this discussion and in this House. Here it is not how long the people are bound to tolerate the illegality of our judgments, but whether we have a right to substitute our occasional opinion in the place of law, so as to deprive the citizen of his franchise.

# SPEECH ON THE POWERS OF JURIES IN PROSECUTIONS FOR LIBELS
## MARCH, 1771

I have always understood that a superintendence over the doctrines, as well as the proceedings, of the courts of justice, was a principal object of the constitution of this House; that you were to watch at once over the lawyer and the law; that there should he an orthodox faith as well as proper works: and I have always looked with a degree of reverence and admiration on this mode of superintendence. For being totally disengaged from the detail of juridical practice, we come to something, perhaps, the better qualified, and certainly much the better disposed to assert the genuine principle of the laws; in which we can, as a body, have no other than an enlarged and a public interest. We have no common cause of a professional attachment, or professional emulations, to bias our minds; we have no foregone opinions, which, from obstinacy and false point of honour, we think ourselves at all events obliged to support. So that with our own minds perfectly disengaged from the exercise, we may superintend the execution of the national justice; which from this circumstance is better secured to the people than in any other country under heaven it can be. As our situation puts us in a proper condition, our power enables us to execute this trust. We may, when we see cause of complaint, administer a remedy; it is in our choice by an address to remove an improper judge, by impeachment before the peers to pursue to destruction a corrupt judge, or by bill to assert, to explain, to enforce, or to reform the law, just as the occasion and necessity of the case shall guide us. We stand in a situation very honourable to ourselves, and very useful to our country, if we do not abuse or abandon the trust that is placed in us.

The question now before you is upon the power of juries in prosecuting for libels. There are four opinions. 1. That the doctrine as held by the courts is proper and constitutional, and therefore should not be altered. 2. That it is neither proper nor constitutional, but that it will be rendered worse by your interference. 3. That it is wrong, but that the only remedy is a bill of retrospect. 4. The opinion of those who bring in the bill; that the thing is wrong, but that it is enough to direct the judgment of the court in future.

The bill brought in is for the purpose of asserting and securing a great object in the juridical constitution of this kingdom; which, from a long series of practices and opinions in our judges, has, in one point, and in one very essential point, deviated from the true principle.

It is the very ancient privilege of the people of England that they shall be tried, except in the known exceptions, not by judges appointed by the Crown, but by their own fellow-subjects, the peers of that county court at which they owe their suit and service; out of this principle trial by juries has grown. This principle has not, that I can find, been contested in any case, by any authority whatsoever; but there is one case, in which, without directly contesting the principle, the whole substance, energy, acid virtue of the privilege, is taken out of it; that is, in the case of a trial by indictment or information for libel. The doctrine in that case laid down by several judges amounts to this, that the jury have no competence where a libel is alleged, except to find the gross corporeal facts of the writing and the publication, together with the identity of the things and persons to which it refers; but that the intent and the tendency of the work, in which intent and tendency the whole criminality consists, is the sole and exclusive province of the judge. Thus having reduced the jury to the cognisance of facts, not in themselves presumptively criminal, but actions neutral and indifferent the whole matter, in which the subject has any concern or interest, is taken out of the hands of the jury: and if the jury take more upon themselves, what they so take is contrary to their duty; it is no moral, but a merely natural power; the same, by which they may do any other improper act, the same, by which they may even prejudice themselves with regard to any other part of the issue before them. Such is the matter as it now stands, in possession of your highest criminal courts, handed down to them from very respectable legal ancestors. If this can once be established in this case, the application in principle to other cases will be easy; and the practice will run upon a descent, until the progress of an encroaching jurisdiction (for it is in its nature to encroach, when once it has passed its limits) coming to confine the juries, case after case, to the corporeal fact, and to that alone, and excluding the intention of mind, the only source of merit and demerit, of reward or punishment, juries become a dead letter in the constitution.

For which reason it is high time to take this matter into the consideration of Parliament, and for that purpose it will be necessary to examine, first, whether there is anything in the peculiar nature of this crime that makes it necessary to exclude the jury from considering the intention in it, more than in others. So far from it, that I take it to be much less so from the analogy of other criminal cases, where no such restraint is ordinarily put upon them. The act of homicide is *primâ facie* criminal. The intention is afterwards to appear, for the jury to acquit or condemn. In burglary do they insist that the jury have nothing to do but to find the taking of goods, and that, if they do, they must necessarily find the party guilty, and leave the rest to the judge; and that they have nothing to do with the word *felonicé* in the indictment?

The next point is to consider it as a question of constitutional policy, that is, whether the decision of the question of libel ought to be left to the judges as a presumption of law, rather than to the jury as matter of popular judgment, as the malice in the case of murder, the felony in the case of stealing. If the intent and tendency are not matters within the province of popular judgment, but legal and technical conclusions, formed upon general principles of law, let us see what they are. Certainly they are most unfavourable, indeed, totally adverse, to the Constitution of this country.

Here we must have recourse to analogies, for we cannot argue on ruled cases one way or the other. See the history. The old books, deficient in general in Crown cases furnish us with little on this head. As to the crime, in the very early Saxon Law, I see an offence of this species, called Folk-leasing, made a capital offence, but no very precise definition of the crime, and no trial at all: see the statute of 3rd Edward I. cap. 34. The law of libels could not have arrived at a very early period in this country. It is no wonder that we find no vestige of any constitution from authority, or of any deductions from legal science in our old books and records upon that subject. The statute of *scandalum magnatum* is the oldest that I know, and this goes but a little way in this sort of learning. Libelling is not the crime of an illiterate people. When they were thought no mean clerks who could read and write, when he who could read and write was presumptively a person in holy orders, libels could not be general or dangerous; and scandals merely oral could spread little, and must perish soon. It is writing, it is printing more emphatically, that imps calumny with those eagle wings, on which, as the poet says, "immortal slanders fly." By the press they spread, they last, they leave the sting in the wound. Printing was not known in England much earlier than the reign of Henry VII., and in the third year of that reign the Court of Star Chamber was established. The press and its enemy are nearly coeval. As no positive law against libels existed, they fell under the indefinite class of misdemeanours. For the trial of misdemeanours that court was instituted, their tendency to produce riots and disorders was a main part of the charge, and was laid, in order to give the court jurisdiction chiefly against libels. The offence was new. Learning of their own upon the subject they had none, and they were obliged to resort to the only emporium where it was to be had, the Roman Law. After the Star Chamber was abolished in the 10th of Charles I. its authority indeed ceased, but its maxims subsisted and survived it. The spirit of the Star Chamber has transmigrated and lived again, and Westminster Hall was obliged to borrow from the Star Chamber, for the same reasons as the Star Chamber had borrowed from the Roman Forum, because they had no law, statute, or tradition of their own. Thus the Roman Law took possession of our courts, I mean its doctrine, not its sanctions; the severity of capital punishment was omitted, all the rest remained. The grounds of these laws are just and equitable. Undoubtedly the good fame of every man ought to be under the protection of the laws as well as his life, and liberty, and property. Good fame is an outwork, that defends them all, and renders them all valuable. The law forbids you to revenge; when it ties up the hands of some, it ought to restrain the tongues of others. The good fame of government is the same, it ought not to be traduced. This is necessary in all government, and if opinion be support, what takes away this destroys that support; but the liberty of the press is necessary to this government.

The wisdom, however, of government is of more importance than the laws. I should study the temper of the people before I ventured on actions of this kind. I would consider the whole of the prosecution of a libel of such importance as Junius, as one piece, as one consistent plan of operations; and I would contrive it so that, if I were defeated, I should not be disgraced; that even my victory should not be more ignominious than my defeat; I would so manage, that the lowest in the predicament of guilt should not be the only one in punishment. I would not inform against the mere vender of a collection of pamphlets. I would not put him to trial first, if I could possibly avoid it. I would rather stand the consequences of my first error, than carry it to a judgment that must disgrace my prosecution, or the court. We ought to examine these things in a manner which becomes ourselves, and becomes the object of the inquiry; not to examine into the most important consideration which can come before us, with minds heated with prejudice and filled with passions, with vain popular opinions and humours, and when we propose to examine into the justice of others, to be unjust ourselves.

An inquiry is wished, as the most effectual way of putting an end to the clamours and libels, which are the disorder and disgrace of the times. For people remain quiet, they sleep secure, when they imagine that the vigilant eye of a censorial magistrate watches over all the proceedings of judicature, and that the sacred fire of an eternal constitutional jealousy, which is the guardian of liberty, law, and justice, is alive night and day, and burning in this house. But when the magistrate gives up his office and his duty, the people assume it, and they inquire too much, and too irreverently, because they think their representatives do not inquire at all.

We have in a libel, 1st. The writing. 2nd. The communication, called by the lawyers the publication. 3rd. The application to persons and facts. 4th. The intent and tendency. 5th. The matter—diminution of fame. The law presumptions on all these are in the communication. No intent can, make a defamatory publication good, nothing can make it have a good tendency; truth is not pleadable. Taken juridically, the foundation of these law presumptions is not unjust; taken constitutionally, they are ruinous, and tend to the total suppression of all publication. If juries are confined to the fact, no writing which censures, however justly, or however temperately, the conduct of administration, can be unpunished. Therefore, if the intent and tendency be left to the judge, as legal conclusions growing from the fact, you may depend upon it you can have no public discussion of a public measure, which is a point which even those who are most offended with the licentiousness of the press (and it is very exorbitant, very provoking) will hardly contend for.

So far as to the first opinion, that the doctrine is right and needs no alteration. 2nd. The next is, that it is wrong, but that we are not in a condition to help it. I admit, it is true, that there are cases of a nature so delicate and complicated, that an Act of Parliament on the subject may become a matter of great difficulty. It sometimes cannot define with exactness, because the subject-matter will not bear an exact definition. It may seem to take away everything which it does not positively establish, and this might be inconvenient; or it may seem *vice versâ* to establish everything which it does not expressly take away. It may be more advisable to leave such matters to the enlightened discretion of a judge, awed by a censorial House of Commons. But then it rests upon those who object to a legislative interposition to prove these inconveniences in the particular case before them. For it would be a most dangerous, as it is a most idle and most groundless, conceit to assume as a general principle, that the rights and liberties of the subject are impaired by the care and attention of the legislature to secure them. If so, very ill would the purchase of Magna Charta have merited the deluge of blood, which was shed in order to have the body of English privileges defined by a positive written law. This charter, the inestimable monument of English freedom, so long the boast and glory of this nation, would have been at once an instrument of our servitude, and a monument of our folly, if this principle were true. The thirty four confirmations would have been only so many repetitions of their absurdity, so many new links in the chain, and so many invalidations of their right.

You cannot open your statute book without seeing positive provisions relative to every right of the subject. This business of juries is the subject of not fewer than a dozen. To suppose that juries are something innate in the Constitution of Great Britain, that they have jumped, like Minerva, out of the head of Jove in complete armour, is a weak fancy, supported neither by precedent nor by reason. Whatever is most ancient and venerable in our Constitution, royal prerogative, privileges of parliament, rights of elections, authority of courts, juries, must have been modelled according to the occasion. I spare your patience, and I pay a compliment to your understanding, in not attempting to prove that anything so elaborate and artificial as a jury was not the work of chance, but a matter of institution, brought to its present state by the joint efforts of legislative authority and juridical prudence. It need not be ashamed of being (what in many parts of it at least it is) the offspring of an Act of Parliament, unless it is a shame for our laws to be the results of our legislature. Juries, which sensitively shrank from the rude touch of parliamentary remedy, have been the subject of not fewer than, I think, forty-three Acts of Parliament, in which they have been changed with all the authority of a creator over its creature, from Magna Charta to the great alterations which were made in the 29th of George II.

To talk of this matter in any other way is to turn a rational principle into an idle and vulgar superstition, like the antiquary, Dr. Woodward, who trembled to have his shield scoured, for fear it should be discovered to be no better than an old pot-lid. This species of tenderness to a jury puts me in mind of a gentleman of good condition, who had been reduced to great poverty and distress; application was made to some rich fellows in his neighbourhood to give him some assistance; but they begged to be excused for fear of affronting a person of his high birth; and so the poor gentleman was left to starve out of pure respect to the antiquity of his family. From this principle has risen an opinion that I find current amongst gentlemen, that this distemper ought to be left to cure itself; that the judges having been well exposed, and something terrified on account of these clamours, will entirely change, if not very much relax from their rigour; if the present race should not change, that the chances of succession may put other more constitutional judges in their place; lastly, if neither should happen, yet that the spirit of an English jury will always be sufficient for the vindication of its own rights, and will not suffer itself to be overborne by the bench. I confess that I totally dissent from all these opinions. These suppositions become the strongest reasons with me to evince the necessity of some clear and positive settlement of this question of contested jurisdiction. If judges are so full of levity, so full of timidity, if they are influenced by such mean and unworthy passions, that a popular clamour is sufficient to shake the resolution they build upon the solid basis of a legal principle, I would endeavour to fix that mercury by a positive law. If to please an administration the judges can go one way to-day, and to please the crowd they can go another to-morrow; if they will oscillate backward and forward between power and popularity, it is high time to fix the law in such a manner as to resemble, as it ought, the great Author of all law, in "whom there is no variableness nor shadow of turning."

As to their succession, I have just the same opinion. I would not leave it to the chances of promotion, or to the characters of lawyers, what the law of the land, what the rights of juries, or what the liberty of the press should be. My law should not depend upon the fluctuation of the closet, or the complexion of men. Whether a black-haired man or a fair-haired man presided in the Court of King's Bench, I would have the law the same: the same whether he was born in *domo regnatrice*, and sucked from his infancy the milk of courts, or was nurtured in the rugged discipline of a popular opposition. This law of court cabal and of party, this *mens quædam nullo perturbata affectu*, this law of complexion, ought not to be endured for a moment in a country whose being depends upon the certainty, clearness, and stability of institutions.

Now I come to the last substitute for the proposed bill, the spirit of juries operating their own jurisdiction. This, I confess, I think the worst of all, for the same reasons on which I objected to the others, and for other weighty reasons besides which are separate and distinct. First, because juries, being taken at random out of a mass of men infinitely large, must be of characters as various as the body they arise from is large in its extent. If the judges differ in their complexions, much more will a jury. A timid jury will give way to an awful judge delivering oracularly the law, and charging them on their oaths, and putting it home to their consciences, to beware of judging where the law had given them no competence. We know that they will do so, they have done so in a hundred instances; a respectable member of your own house, no vulgar man, tells you that on the authority of a judge he found a man guilty, in whom, at the same time, he could find no guilt. But supposing them full of knowledge and full of manly confidence in themselves, how will their knowledge, or their confidence, inform or inspirit others? They give no reason for their verdict, they can but condemn or acquit; and no man can tell the motives on which they have acquitted or condemned. So that this hope of the power of juries to assert their own jurisdiction must be a principle blind, as being without reason, and as changeable as the complexion of men and the temper of the times.

But, after all, is it fit that this dishonourable contention between the court and juries should subsist any longer? On what principle is it that a jury refuses to be directed by the court as to his competence? Whether a libel or no libel be a question of law or of fact may be doubted, but a question of jurisdiction and competence is certainly a question of law; on this the court ought undoubtedly to judge, and to judge solely and exclusively. If they judge wrong from excusable error, you ought to correct it, as to-day it is proposed, by an explanatory bill; or if by corruption, by bill of penalties declaratory, and by punishment. What does a juror say to a judge when he refuses his opinion upon a question of judicature? You are so corrupt, that I should consider myself a partaker of your crime, were I to be guided by your opinion; or you are so grossly ignorant, that I, fresh from my bounds, from my plough, my counter, or my loom, am fit to direct you in your profession. This is an unfitting, it is a dangerous, state of things. The spirit of any sort of men is not a fit rule for deciding on the bounds of their jurisdiction. First, because it is different in different men, and even different in the same at different times; and can never become the proper directing line of law; next, because it is not reason, but feeling; and when once it is irritated, it is not apt to confine itself within its proper limits. If it becomes, not difference in opinion upon law, but a trial of spirit between parties, our courts of law are no longer the temple of justice, but the amphitheatre for gladiators. No—God forbid! Juries ought to take their law from the bench only; but it is our business that they should hear nothing from the bench but what is agreeable to the principles of the Constitution. The jury are to hear the judge, the judge is to hear the law where it speaks plain; where it does not, he is to hear the legislature. As I do not think these opinions of the judges to be agreeable to those principles, I wish to take the only method in which they can or ought to be corrected, by bill.

Next, my opinion is, that it ought to be rather by a bill for removing controversies than by a bill in the state of manifest and express declaration, and in words *de præterito*. I do this upon reasons of equity and constitutional policy. I do not want to censure the present judges. I think them to be excused for their error. Ignorance is no excuse for a judge: it is changing the nature of his crime—it is not absolving. It must be such error as a wise and conscientious judge may possibly fall into, and must arise from one or both these causes: first, a plausible principle of law; secondly, the precedents of respectable authorities, and in good times. In the first, the principle of law, that the judge is to decide on law, the jury to decide on fact, is an ancient and venerable principle and maxim of the law, and if supported in this application by precedents of good times and of good men, the judge, if wrong, ought to be corrected; he ought not to be reproved, or to be disgraced, or the authority or respect to your tribunals to be impaired. In cases in which declaratory bills have been made, where by violence and corruption some fundamental part of the Constitution has been struck at; where they would damn the principle, censure the persons, and annul the acts; but where the law having been, by the accident of human frailty, depraved, or in a particular instance misunderstood, where you neither mean to rescind the acts, nor to censure the persons, in such cases you have taken the explanatory mode, and, without condemning what is done, you direct the future judgment of the court.

All bills for the reformation of the law must be according to the subject-matter, the circumstances, and the occasion, and are of four kinds:— 1. Either the law is totally wanting, and then a new enacting statute must be made to supply that want; or, 2. It is defective, then a new law must be made to enforce it. 3. Or it is opposed by power or fraud, and then an act must be made to declare it. 4 Or it is rendered doubtful and controverted, and then a law must be made to explain it. These must be applied according to the exigence of the case; one is just as good as another of them. Miserable, indeed, would be the resources, poor and unfurnished the stores and magazines of legislation, if we were bound up to a little narrow form, and not able to frame our acts of parliament according to every disposition of our own minds, and to every possible emergency of the commonwealth; to make them declaratory, enforcing, explanatory, repealing, just in what mode, or in what degree we please.

Those who think that the judges, living and dead, are to be condemned, that your tribunals of justice are to be dishonoured, that their acts and judgments on this business are to be rescinded, they will undoubtedly vote against this bill, and for another sort.

I am not of the opinion of those gentlemen who are against disturbing the public repose; I like a clamour whenever there is an abuse. The fire-bell at midnight disturbs your sleep, but it keeps you from being burned in your bed. The hue and cry alarms the county, but it preserves all the property of the province. All these clamours aim at redress. But a clamour made merely for the purpose of rendering the people discontented with their situation, without an endeavour to give them a practical remedy, is indeed one of the worst acts of sedition.

I have read and heard much upon the conduct of our courts in the business of libels. I was extremely willing to enter into, and very free to act as facts should turn out on that inquiry, aiming constantly at remedy as the end of all clamour, all debate, all writing, and all inquiry; for which reason I did embrace, and do now with joy, this method of giving quiet to the courts, jurisdiction to juries, liberty to the press, and satisfaction to the people. I thank my friends for what they have done; I hope the public will one day reap the benefit of their pious and judicious endeavours. They have now sown the seed; I hope they will live to see the flourishing harvest. Their bill is sown in weakness; it will, I trust, be reaped in power; and then, however, we shall have reason to apply to them what my Lord Coke says was an aphorism continually in the mouth of a great sage of the law, "Blessed be not the complaining tongue, but blessed be the amending hand."

# SPEECH ON A BILL FOR SHORTENING THE DURATION OF PARLIAMENTS

It is always to be lamented when men are driven to search into the foundations of the commonwealth. It is certainly necessary to resort to the theory of your government whenever you propose any alteration in the frame of it, whether that alteration means the revival of some former antiquated and forsaken constitution of state, or the introduction of some new improvement in the commonwealth. The object of our deliberation is, to promote the good purposes for which elections have been instituted, and to prevent their inconveniences. If we thought frequent elections attended with no inconvenience, or with but a trifling inconvenience, the strong overruling principle of the Constitution would sweep us like a torrent towards them. But your remedy is to be suited to your disease—your present disease, and to your whole disease. That man thinks much too highly, and therefore he thinks weakly and delusively, of any contrivance of human wisdom, who believes that it can make any sort of approach to perfection. There is not, there never was, a principle of government under heaven, that does not, in the very pursuit of the good it proposes, naturally and inevitably lead into some inconvenience, which makes it absolutely necessary to counterwork and weaken the application of that first principle itself; and to abandon something of the extent of the advantage you proposed by it, in order to prevent also the inconveniences which have arisen from the instrument of all the good you had in view.

To govern according to the sense and agreeably to the interests of the people is a great and glorious object of government. This object cannot be obtained but through the medium of popular election, and popular election is a mighty evil. It is such, and so great an evil, that though there are few nations whose monarchs were not originally elective, very few are now elected. They are the distempers of elections, that have destroyed all free states. To cure these distempers is difficult, if not impossible; the only thing therefore left to save the commonwealth is to prevent their return too frequently. The objects in view are, to have parliaments as frequent as they can be without distracting them in the prosecution of public business; on one hand, to secure their dependence upon the people, on the other to give them that quiet in their minds, and that ease in their fortunes, as to enable them to perform the most arduous and most painful duty in the world with spirit, with efficiency, with independency, and with experience, as real public counsellors, not as the canvassers at a perpetual election. It is wise to compass as many good ends as possibly you can, and seeing there are inconveniences on both sides, with benefits on both, to give up a part of the benefit to soften the inconvenience. The perfect cure is impracticable, because the disorder is dear to those from whom alone the cure can possibly be derived. The utmost to be done is to palliate, to mitigate, to respite, to put off the evil day of the Constitution to its latest possible hour, and may it be a very late one!

This bill, I fear, would precipitate one of two consequences, I know not which most likely, or which most dangerous: either that the Crown by its constant stated power, influence, and revenue, would wear out all opposition in elections, or that a violent and furious popular spirit would arise. I must see, to satisfy me, the remedies; I must see, from their operation in the cure of the old evil, and in the cure of those new evils, which are inseparable from all remedies, how they balance each other, and what is the total result. The excellence of mathematics and metaphysics is to have but one thing before you, but he forms the best judgment in all moral disquisitions, who has the greatest number and variety of considerations, in one view before him, and can take them in with the best possible consideration of the middle results of all.

We of the opposition, who are not friends to the bill, give this pledge at least of our integrity and sincerity to the people, that in our situation of systematic opposition to the present ministers, in which all our hope of rendering it effectual depends upon popular interest and favour, we will not flatter them by a surrender of our uninfluenced judgment and opinion; we give a security, that if ever we should be in another situation, no flattery to any other sort of power and influence would induce us to act against the true interests of the people.

All are agreed that parliaments should not be perpetual; the only question is, what is the most convenient time for their duration? On which there are three opinions. We are agreed, too, that the term ought not to be chosen most likely in its operation to spread corruption, and to augment the already overgrown influence of the crown. On these principles I mean to debate the question. It is easy to pretend a zeal for liberty. Those who think themselves not likely to be encumbered with the performance of their promises, either from their known inability, or total indifference about the performance, never fail to entertain the most lofty ideas. They are certainly the most specious, and they cost them neither reflection to frame, nor pains to modify, nor management to support. The task is of another nature to those who mean to promise nothing that it is not in their intentions, or may possibly be in their power to perform; to those who are bound and principled no more to delude the understandings than to violate the liberty of their fellow-subjects. Faithful watchmen we ought to be over the rights and privileges of the people. But our duty, if we are qualified for it as we ought, is to give them information, and not to receive it from them; we are not to go to school to them to learn the principles of law and government. In doing so we should not dutifully serve, but we should basely and scandalously betray, the people, who are not capable of this service by nature, nor in any instance called to it by the Constitution. I reverentially look up to the opinion of the people, and with an awe that is almost superstitious. I should be ashamed to show my face before them, if I changed my ground, as they cried up or cried down men, or things, or opinions; if I wavered and shifted about with every change, and joined in it, or opposed, as best answered any low interest or passion; if I held them up hopes, which I knew I never intended, or promised what I well knew I could not perform. Of all these things they are perfect sovereign judges without appeal; but as to the detail of particular measures, or to any general schemes of policy, they have neither enough of speculation in the closet, nor of experience in business, to decide upon it. They can well see whether we are tools of a court, or their honest servants. Of that they can well judge; and I wish that they always exercised their judgment; but of the particular merits of a measure I have other standards. That the frequency of elections proposed by this bill has a tendency to increase the power and consideration of the electors, not lessen corruptibility, I do most readily allow; so far as it is desirable, this is what it has; I will tell you now what it has not: 1st. It has no sort of tendency to increase their integrity and public spirit, unless an increase of power has an operation upon voters in elections, that it has in no other situation in the world, and upon no other part of mankind. 2nd. This bill has no tendency to limit the quantity of influence in the Crown, to render its operation more difficult, or to counteract that operation, which it cannot prevent, in any way whatsoever. It has its full weight, its full range, and its uncontrolled operation on the electors exactly as it had before. 3rd. Nor, thirdly, does it abate the interest or inclination of Ministers to apply that influence to the electors: on the contrary, it renders it much more necessary to them, if they seek to have a majority in parliament, to increase the means of that influence, and redouble their diligence, and to sharpen dexterity in the application. The whole effect of the bill is therefore the removing the application of some part of the influence from the elected to the electors, and further to strengthen and extend a court interest already great and powerful in boroughs; here to fix their magazines and places of arms, and thus to make them the principal, not the secondary, theatre of their manoeuvres for securing a determined majority in parliament.

I believe nobody will deny that the electors are corruptible. They are men; it is saying nothing worse of them; many of them are but ill-informed in their minds, many feeble in their circumstances, easily over-reached, easily seduced. If they are many, the wages of corruption are the lower; and would to God it were not rather a contemptible and hypocritical adulation than a charitable sentiment, to say that there is already no debauchery, no corruption, no bribery, no perjury, no blind fury, and interested faction among the electors in many parts of this kingdom: nor is it surprising, or at all blamable, in that class of private men, when they see their neighbours aggrandised, and themselves poor and virtuous, without that *éclat* or dignity which attends men in higher stations.

But admit it were true that the great mass of the electors were too vast an object for court influence to grasp, or extend to, and that in despair they must abandon it; he must be very ignorant of the state of every popular interest, who does not know that in all the corporations, all the open boroughs—indeed, in every district of the kingdom—there is some leading man, some agitator, some wealthy merchant, or considerable manufacturer, some active attorney, some popular preacher, some money-lender, &c., &c., who is followed by the whole flock. This is the style of all free countries.

> —Multùm in Fabiâ valet hic, valet ille Velinâ;
> Cuilibet hic fasces dabit eripietque curule.

These spirits, each of which informs and governs his own little orb, are neither so many, nor so little powerful, nor so incorruptible, but that a Minister may, as he does frequently, find means of gaining them, and through them all their followers. To establish, therefore, a very general influence among electors will no more be found an impracticable project, than to gain an undue influence over members of parliament. Therefore I am apprehensive that this bill, though it shifts the place of the disorder, does by no means relieve the Constitution. I went through almost every contested election in the beginning of this parliament, and acted as a manager in very many of them: by which, though at a school of pretty severe and ragged discipline, I came to have some degree of instruction concerning the means by which parliamentary interests are in general procured and supported.

Theory, I know, would suppose, that every general election is to the representative a day of judgment, in which he appears before his constituents to account for the use of the talent with which they entrusted him, and of the improvement he had made of it for the public advantage. It would be so, if every corruptible representative were to find an enlightened and incorruptible constituent. But the practice and knowledge of the world will not suffer us to be ignorant, that the Constitution on paper is one thing, and in fact and experience is another. We must know that the candidate, instead of trusting at his election to the testimony of his behaviour in parliament, must bring the testimony of a large sum of money, the capacity of liberal expense in entertainments, the power of serving and obliging the rulers of corporations, of winning over the popular leaders of political clubs, associations, and neighbourhoods. It is ten thousand times more necessary to show himself a man of power, than a man of integrity, in almost all the elections with which I have been acquainted. Elections, therefore, become a matter of heavy expense; and if contests are frequent, to many they will become a matter of an expense totally ruinous, which no fortunes can bear;

but least of all the landed fortunes, encumbered as they often, indeed as they mostly are, with debts, with portions, with jointures; and tied up in the hands of the possessor by the limitations of settlement. It is a material, it is in my opinion a lasting, consideration, in all the questions concerning election. Let no one think the charges of election a trivial matter.

The charge, therefore, of elections ought never to be lost sight of, in a question concerning their frequency, because the grand object you seek is independence. Independence of mind will ever be more or less influenced by independence of fortune; and if, every three years, the exhausting sluices of entertainments, drinkings, open houses, to say nothing of bribery, are to be periodically drawn up and renewed—if government favours, for which now, in some shape or other, the whole race of men are candidates, are to be called for upon every occasion, I see that private fortunes will be washed away, and every, even to the least, trace of independence, borne down by the torrent. I do not seriously think this Constitution, even to the wrecks of it, could survive five triennial elections. If you are to fight the battle, you must put on the armour of the Ministry; you must call in the public, to the aid of private, money. The expense of the last election has been computed (and I am persuaded that it has not been overrated) at £1,500,000; three shillings in the pound more on the Land Tax. About the close of the last Parliament, and the beginning of this, several agents for boroughs went about, and I remember well that it was in every one of their mouths—"Sir, your election will cost you three thousand pounds, if you are independent; but if the Ministry supports you, it may be done for two, and perhaps for less;" and, indeed, the thing spoke itself. Where a living was to be got for one, a commission in the army for another, a post in the navy for a third, and Custom-house offices scattered about without measure or number, who doubts but money may be saved? The Treasury may even add money; but, indeed, it is superfluous. A gentleman of two thousand a year, who meets another of the same fortune, fights with equal arms; but if to one of the candidates you add a thousand a year in places for himself, and a power of giving away as much among others, one must, or there is no truth in arithmetical demonstration, ruin his adversary, if he is to meet him and to fight with him every third year. It will be said, I do not allow for the operation of character; but I do; and I know it will have its weight in most elections; perhaps it may be decisive in some. But there are few in which it will prevent great expenses.

The destruction of independent fortunes will be the consequence on the part of the candidate. What will be the consequence of triennial corruption, triennial drunkenness, triennial idleness, triennial law-suits, litigations, prosecutions, triennial frenzy; of society dissolved, industry interrupted, ruined; of those personal hatreds that will never be suffered to soften; those animosities and feuds, which will be rendered immortal; those quarrels, which are never to be appeased; morals vitiated and gangrened to the vitals? I think no stable and useful advantages were ever made by the money got at elections by the voter, but all he gets is doubly lost to the public; it is money given to diminish the general stock of the community, which is the industry of the subject. I am sure that it is a good while before he or his family settle again to their business. Their heads will never cool; the temptations of elections will be for ever glittering before their eyes. They will all grow politicians; every one, quitting his business, will choose to enrich himself by his vote. They will take the gauging-rod; new places will be made for them; they will run to the Custom-house quay, their looms and ploughs will be deserted.

So was Rome destroyed by the disorders of continual elections, though those of Rome were sober disorders. They had nothing but faction, bribery, bread, and stage plays to debauch them. We have the inflammation of liquor superadded, a fury hotter than any of them. There the contest was only between citizen and citizen; here you have the contests of ambitious citizens on one side, supported by the Crown, to oppose to the efforts (let it be so) of private and unsupported ambition on the other. Yet Rome was destroyed by the frequency and charge of elections, and the monstrous expense of an unremitted courtship to the people. I think, therefore, the independent candidate and elector may each be destroyed by it, the whole body of the community be an infinite sufferer, and a vicious Ministry the only gainer. Gentlemen, I know, feel the weight of this argument; they agree that this would be the consequence of more frequent elections, if things were to continue as they are. But they think the greatness and frequency of the evil would itself be a remedy for it; that, sitting but for a short time, the member would not find it worth while to make such vast expenses, while the fear of their constituents will hold them the more effectually to their duty.

To this I answer, that experience is full against them. This is no new thing; we have had triennial parliaments; at no period of time were seats more eagerly contested. The expenses of elections ran higher, taking the state of all charges, than they do now. The expense of entertainments was such, that an Act, equally severe and ineffectual, was made against it; every monument of the time bears witness of the expense, and most of the Acts against corruption in elections were then made; all the writers talked of it and lamented it. Will any one think that a corporation will be contented with a bowl of punch, or a piece of beef the less, because elections are every three, instead of every seven years? Will they change their wine for ale, because they are to get more ale three years hence? Do not think it. Will they make fewer demands for the advantages of patronage in favours and offices, because their member is brought more under their power? We have not only our own historical experience in England upon this subject, but we have the experience co-existing with us in Ireland, where, since their Parliament has been shortened, the expense of elections has been so far from being lowered that it has been very near doubled. Formerly they sat for the king's life; the ordinary charge of a seat in Parliament was then £1,500. They now sit eight years, four sessions: it is now £2,500 and upwards. The spirit of emulation has also been extremely increased, and all who are acquainted with the tone of that country have no doubt that the spirit is still growing, that new candidates will take the field, that the contests will be more violent, and the expenses of elections larger than ever.

It never can be otherwise. A seat in this House, for good purposes, for bad purposes, for no purpose at all (except the mere consideration derived from being concerned in the public councils) will ever be a first-rate object of ambition in England. Ambition is no exact calculator. Avarice itself does not calculate strictly when it games. One thing is certain, that in this political game the great lottery of power is that into which men will purchase with millions of chances against them. In Turkey, where the place, where the fortune, where the head itself, are so insecure, that scarcely any have died in their beds for ages, so that the bowstring is the natural death of Bashaws, yet in no country is power and distinction (precarious enough, God knows, in all) sought for with such boundless avidity, as if the value of place was enhanced by the danger and insecurity of its tenure. Nothing will ever make a seat in this House not an object of desire to numbers by any means or at any charge, but the depriving it of all power and all dignity. This would do it. This is the true and only nostrum for that purpose. But a House of Commons without power and without dignity, either in itself or its members, is no House of Commons for the purposes of this Constitution.

But they will be afraid to act ill, if they know that the day of their account is always near. I wish it were true, but it is not; here again we have experience, and experience is against us. The distemper of this age is a poverty of spirit and of genius; it is trifling, it is futile, worse than ignorant, superficially taught, with the politics and morals of girls at a boarding-school, rather than of men and statesmen; but it is not yet desperately wicked, or so scandalously venal as in former times. Did not a triennial parliament give up the national dignity, approve the Peace of Utrecht, and almost give up everything else in taking every step to defeat the Protestant succession? Was not the Constitution saved by those who had no election at all to go to, the Lords, because the Court applied to electors, and by various means carried them from their true interests; so that the Tory Ministry had a majority without an application to a single member? Now, as to the conduct of the members, it was then far from pure and independent. Bribery was infinitely more flagrant. A predecessor of yours, Mr. Speaker, put the question of his own expulsion for bribery. Sir William Musgrave was a wise man, a grave man, an independent man, a man of good fortune and good family; however, he carried on while in opposition a traffic, a shameful traffic with the Ministry. Bishop Burnet knew of £6,000 which he had received at one payment. I believe the payment of sums in hard money—plain, naked bribery—is rare amongst us. It was then far from uncommon.

A triennial was near ruining, a septennial parliament saved, your Constitution; nor perhaps have you ever known a more flourishing period for the union of national prosperity, dignity, and liberty, than the sixty years you have passed under that Constitution of parliament.

The shortness of time, in which they are to reap the profits of iniquity, is far from checking the avidity of corrupt men; it renders them infinitely more ravenous. They rush violently and precipitately on their object, they lose all regard to decorum. The moments of profit are precious; never are men so wicked as during a general mortality. It was so in the great plague at Athens, every symptom of which (and this its worst amongst the rest) is so finely related by a great historian of antiquity. It was so in the plague of London in 1665. It appears in soldiers, sailors, &c. Whoever would contrive to render the life of man much shorter than it is, would, I am satisfied, find the surest recipe for increasing the wickedness of our nature.

Thus, in my opinion, the shortness of a triennial sitting would have the following ill effects:—It would make the member more shamelessly and shockingly corrupt, it would increase his dependence on those who could best support him at his election, it would wrack and tear to pieces the fortunes of those who stood upon their own fortunes and their private interest, it would make the electors infinitely more venal, and it would make the whole body of the people, who are, whether they have votes or not, concerned in elections, more lawless, more idle, more debauched; it would utterly destroy the sobriety, the industry, the integrity, the simplicity of all the people, and undermine, I am much afraid, the deepest and best laid foundations of the commonwealth.

Those who have spoken and written upon this subject without doors, do not so much deny the probable existence of these inconveniences in their measure, as they trust for the prevention to remedies of various sorts, which they propose. First, a place bill; but if this will not do, as they fear it will not, then, they say, we will have a rotation, and a certain number of you shall be rendered incapable of being elected for ten years. Then, for the electors, they shall ballot; the members of parliament also shall decide by ballot; and a fifth project is the change of the present legal representation of the kingdom. On all this I shall observe, that it will be very unsuitable to your wisdom to adopt the project of a bill, to which there are objections insuperable by anything in the bill itself, upon the hope that those objections may be removed by subsequent projects; every one of which is full of difficulties of its own, and which are all of them very essential alterations in the Constitution. This seems very irregular and unusual. If anything should make this a very doubtful measure, what can make it more so than that, in the opinion of its advocates, it would aggravate all our old inconveniences in such a manner as to require a total alteration in the Constitution of the kingdom? If the remedies are proper in a triennial, they will not be less so in septennial elections; let us try them first, see how the House relishes them, see how they will operate in the nation; and then, having felt your way, you will be prepared against these inconveniences.

The honourable gentleman sees that I respect the principle upon which he goes, as well as his intentions and his abilities. He will believe that I do not differ from him wantonly, and on trivial grounds. He is very sure that it was not his embracing one way which determined me to take the other. I have not, in newspapers, to derogate from his fair fame with the nation, printed the first rude sketch of his bill with ungenerous and invidious comments. I have not, in conversations industriously circulated about the town, and talked on the benches of this House, attributed his conduct to motives low and unworthy, and as groundless as they are injurious. I do not affect to be frightened with this proposition, as if some hideous spectre had started from hell, which was to be sent back again by every form of exorcism, and every kind of incantation. I invoke no Acheron to overwhelm him in the whirlpools of his muddy gulf. I do not tell the respectable mover and seconder, by a perversion of their sense and expressions, that their proposition halts between the ridiculous and the dangerous. I am not one of those who start up three at a time, and fall upon and strike at him with so much eagerness, that our daggers hack one another in his sides. My honourable friend has not brought down a spirited imp of chivalry, to win the first achievement and blazon of arms on his milk-white shield in a field listed against him, nor brought out the generous offspring of lions, and said to them, "Not against that side of the forest, beware of that—here is the prey where you are to fasten your paws;" and seasoning his unpractised jaws with blood, tell him, "This is the milk for which you are to thirst hereafter." We furnish at his expense no holiday, nor suspend hell that a crafty Ixion may have rest from his wheel; nor give the common adversary, if he be a common adversary, reason to say, "I would have put in my word to oppose, but the eagerness of your allies in your social war was such that I could not break in upon you." I hope he sees and feels, and that every member sees and feels along with him, the difference between amicable dissent and civil discord.

# SPEECH ON REFORM OF REPRESENTATION IN THE HOUSE OF COMMONS
## JUNE, 1784

Mr. Speaker,—We have now discovered, at the close of the eighteenth century, that the Constitution of England, which for a series of ages had been the proud distinction of this country, always the admiration, and sometimes the envy, of the wise and learned in every other nation—we have discovered that this boasted Constitution, in the most boasted part of it, is a gross imposition upon the understanding of mankind, an insult to their feelings, and acting by contrivances destructive to the best and most valuable interests of the people. Our political architects have taken a survey of the fabric of the British Constitution. It is singular that they report nothing against the Crown, nothing against the Lords; but in the House of Commons everything is unsound; it is ruinous in every part. It is infested by the dry rot, and ready to tumble about our ears without their immediate help. You know by the faults they find what are their ideas of the alteration. As all government stands upon opinion, they know that the way utterly to destroy it is to remove that opinion, to take away all reverence, all confidence from it; and then, at the first blast of public discontent and popular tumult, it tumbles to the ground.

In considering this question, they who oppose it, oppose it on different grounds; one is in the nature of a previous question—that some alterations may be expedient, but that this is not the time for making them. The other is, that no essential alterations are at all wanting, and that neither now, nor at any time, is it prudent or safe to be meddling with the fundamental principles and ancient tried usages of our Constitution—that our representation is as nearly perfect as the necessary imperfection of human affairs and of human creatures will suffer it to be; and that it is a subject of prudent and honest use and thankful enjoyment, and not of captious criticism and rash experiment.

On the other side, there are two parties, who proceed on two grounds—in my opinion, as they state them, utterly irreconcilable. The one is juridical, the other political. The one is in the nature of a claim of right, on the supposed rights of man as man; this party desire the decision of a suit. The other ground, as far as I can divine what it directly means, is, that the representation is not so politically framed as to answer the theory of its institution. As to the claim of right, the meanest petitioner, the most gross and ignorant, is as good as the best; in some respects his claim is more favourable on account of his ignorance; his weakness, his poverty and distress only add to his titles; he sues *in formâ pauperis*: he ought to be a favourite of the Court. But when the other ground is taken, when the question is political, when a new Constitution is to be made on a sound theory of government, then the presumptuous pride of didactic ignorance is to be excluded from the council in this high and arduous matter, which often bids defiance to the experience of the wisest. The first claims a personal representation; the latter rejects it with scorn and fervour. The language of the first party is plain and intelligible; they who plead an absolute right, cannot be satisfied with anything short of personal representation, because all natural rights must be the rights of individuals: as by nature there is no such thing as politic or corporate personality; all these ideas are mere fictions of law, they are creatures of voluntary institution; men as men are individuals, and nothing else. They, therefore, who reject the principle of natural and personal representation, are essentially and eternally at variance with those who claim it. As to the first sort of reformers, it is ridiculous to talk to them of the British Constitution upon any or all of its bases; for they lay it down, that every man ought to govern himself, and that where he cannot go himself he must send his representative; that all other government is usurpation, and is so far from having a claim to our obedience, that it is not only our right, but our duty, to resist it. Nine-tenths of the reformers argue thus—that is, on the natural right. It is impossible not to make some reflection on the nature of this claim, or avoid a comparison between the extent of the principle and the present object of the demand. If this claim be founded, it is clear to what it goes. The House of Commons, in that light, undoubtedly is no representative of the people as a collection of individuals. Nobody pretends it, nobody can justify such an assertion. When you come to examine into this claim of right, founded on the right of self-government in each individual, you find the thing demanded infinitely short of the principle of the demand. What! one-third only of the legislature, of the government no share at all? What sort of treaty of partition is this for those who have no inherent right to the whole? Give them all they ask, and your grant is still a cheat; for how comes only a third to be their younger children's fortune in this settlement? How came they neither to have the choice of kings, or lords, or judges, or generals, or admirals, or bishops, or priests, or ministers, or justices of peace? Why, what have you to answer in favour of the prior rights of the Crown and peerage but this—our Constitution is a proscriptive Constitution; it is a Constitution whose sole authority is, that it has existed time out of mind. It is settled in these two portions against one, legislatively; and in the whole of the judicature, the whole of the federal capacity, of the executive, the prudential and the financial administration, in one alone. Nor were your House of Lords and the prerogatives of the Crown settled on any adjudication in favour of natural rights, for they could never be so portioned. Your king, your lords, your judges, your juries, grand and little, all are prescriptive; and what proves it is the disputes not yet concluded, and never near becoming so, when any of them first originated. Prescription is the most solid of all titles, not only to property, but, which is to secure that property, to government. They harmonise with each other, and give mutual aid to one another. It is accompanied with another ground of authority in the constitution of the human mind—presumption. It is a presumption in favour of any settled scheme of government against any untried project, that a nation has long existed and flourished under it. It is a better presumption even of the choice of a nation, far better than any sudden and temporary arrangement by actual election. Because a nation is not an idea only of local extent, and individual momentary aggregation, but it is an idea of continuity, which extends in time as well as in numbers and in space. And this is a choice not of one day, or one set of people, not a tumultuary and giddy choice; it is a deliberate election of ages and of generations; it is a Constitution made by what is ten thousand times better than choice—it is made by the peculiar circumstances, occasions, tempers, dispositions, and moral, civil, and social habitudes of the people, which disclose themselves only in a long space of time. It is a vestment, which accommodates itself to the body. Nor is prescription of government formed upon blind, unmeaning prejudices—for man is a most unwise, and a most wise being. The individual is foolish. The multitude, for the moment, are foolish, when they act without deliberation; but the species is wise, and when time is given to it, as a species it almost always acts right.

The reason for the Crown as it is, for the Lords as they are, is my reason for the Commons as they are, the electors as they are. Now, if the Crown and the Lords, and the judicatures, are all prescriptive, so is the House of Commons of the very same origin, and of no other. We and our electors have powers and privileges both made and circumscribed by prescription, as much to the full as the other parts; and as such we have always claimed them, and on no other title. The House of Commons is a legislative body corporate by prescription, not made upon any given theory, but existing prescriptively—just like the rest. This prescription has made it essentially what it is—an aggregate collection of three parts—knights, citizens, burgesses. The question is, whether this has been always so, since the House of Commons has taken its present shape and circumstances, and has been an essential operative part of the Constitution; which, I take it, it has been for at least five hundred years.

This I resolve to myself in the affirmative: and then another question arises; whether this House stands firm upon its ancient foundations, and is not, by time and accidents, so declined from its perpendicular as to want the hand of the wise and experienced architects of the day to set it upright again, and to prop and buttress it up for duration;—whether it continues true to the principles upon which it has hitherto stood;—whether this be *de facto* the Constitution of the House of Commons as it has been since the time that the House of Commons has, without dispute, become a necessary and an efficient part of the British Constitution? To ask whether a thing, which has always been the same, stands to its usual principle, seems to me to be perfectly absurd; for how do you know the principles but from the construction? and if that remains the same, the principles remain the same. It is true, that to say your Constitution is what it has been, is no sufficient defence for those who say it is a bad Constitution. It is an answer to those who say that it is a degenerate Constitution. To those who say it is a bad one, I answer, Look to its effects. In all moral machinery the moral results are its test.

On what grounds do we go to restore our Constitution to what it has been at some given period, or to reform and reconstruct it upon principles more conformable to a sound theory of government? A prescriptive government, such as ours, never was the work of any legislator, never was made upon any foregone theory. It seems to me a preposterous way of reasoning, and a perfect confusion of ideas, to take the theories, which learned and speculative men have made from that government, and then, supposing it made on these theories, which were made from it, to accuse the government as not corresponding with them. I do not vilify theory and speculation—no, because that would be to vilify reason itself. "*Neque decipitur ratio, neque decipit unquam.*" No; whenever I speak against theory, I mean always a weak, erroneous, fallacious, unfounded, or imperfect theory; and one of the ways of discovering that it is a false theory is by comparing it with practice. This is the true touchstone of all theories which regard man and the affairs of men: Does it suit his nature in general?—does it suit his nature as modified by his habits?

The more frequently this affair is discussed, the stronger the case appears to the sense and the feelings of mankind. I have no more doubt than I entertain of my existence, that this very thing, which is stated as a horrible thing, is the means of the preservation of our Constitution whilst it lasts: of curing it of many of the disorders which, attending every species of institution, would attend the principle of an exact local representation, or a representation on the principle of numbers. If you reject personal representation, you are pushed upon expedience; and then what they wish us to do is, to prefer their speculations on that subject to the happy experience of this country of a growing liberty and a growing prosperity for five hundred years. Whatever respect I have for their talents, this, for one, I will not do. Then what is the standard of expedience? Expedience is that which is good for the community, and good for every individual in it. Now this expedience is the *desideratum* to be sought, either without the experience of means, or with that experience. If without, as in the case of the fabrication of a new commonwealth, I will hear the learned arguing what promises to be expedient; but if we are to judge of a commonwealth actually existing, the first thing I inquire is, What has been found expedient or inexpedient? And I will not take their promise rather than the performance of the Constitution.

But no; this was not the cause of the discontents. I went through most of the northern parts—the Yorkshire election was then raging; the year before, through most of the western counties—Bath, Bristol, Gloucester—not one word, either in the towns or country, on the subject of representation; much on the receipt tax, something on Mr. Fox's ambition; much greater apprehension of danger from thence than from want of representation. One would think that the ballast of the ship was shifted with us, and that our Constitution had the gunnel under water. But can you fairly and distinctly point out what one evil or grievance has happened, which you can refer to the representative not following the opinion of his constituents? What one symptom do we find of this inequality? But it is not an arithmetical inequality with which we ought to trouble ourselves. If there be a moral, a political equality, this is the *desideratum* in our Constitution, and in every Constitution in the world. Moral inequality is as between places and between classes. Now, I ask, what advantage do you find, that the places which abound in representation possess over others in which it is more scanty, in security for freedom, in security for justice, or in any one of those means of procuring temporal prosperity and eternal happiness, the ends for which society was formed? Are the local interests of Cornwall and Wiltshire, for instance—their roads, canals, their prisons, their police—better than Yorkshire, Warwickshire, or Staffordshire? Warwick has members; is Warwick or Stafford more opulent, happy, or free, than Newcastle or than Birmingham? Is Wiltshire the pampered favourite, whilst Yorkshire, like the child of the bondwoman, is turned out to the desert? This is like the unhappy persons who live, if they can be said to live, in the statical chair; who are ever feeling their pulse, and who do not judge of health by the aptitude of the body to perform its functions, but by their ideas of what ought to be the true balance between the several secretions. Is a committee of Cornwall, &c., thronged, and the others deserted? No. You have an equal representation, because you have men equally interested in the prosperity of the whole, who are involved in the general interest and the general sympathy; and perhaps these places, furnishing a superfluity of public agents and administrators (whether, in strictness, they are representatives or not, I do not mean to inquire, but they are agents and administrators), will stand clearer of local interests, passions, prejudices, and cabals than the others, and therefore preserve the balance of the parts, and with a more general view and a more steady hand than the rest.

In every political proposal we must not leave out of the question the political views and object of the proposer; and these we discover, not by what he says, but by the principles he lays down. "I mean," says he, "a moderate and temperate reform;" that is, "I mean to do as little good as possible. If the Constitution be what you represent it, and there be no danger in the change, you do wrong not to make the reform commensurate to the abuse." Fine reformer, indeed! generous donor! What is the cause of this parsimony of the liberty which you dole out to the people? Why all this limitation in giving blessings and benefits to mankind? You admit that there is an extreme in liberty, which may be infinitely noxious to those who are to receive it, and which in the end will leave them no liberty at all. I think so too; they know it, and they feel it. The question is, then, What is the standard of that extreme? What that gentleman, and the associations, or some parts of their phalanxes, think proper. Then our liberties are in their pleasure; it depends on their arbitrary will how far I shall be free. I will have none of that freedom. If, therefore, the standard of moderation be sought for, I will seek for it. Where? Not in their fancies, nor in my own: I will seek for it where I know it is to be found—in the Constitution I actually enjoy. Here it says to an encroaching prerogative—"Your sceptre has its length; you cannot add a hair to your head, or a gem to your crown, but what an eternal law has given to it." Here it says to an overweening peerage—"Your pride finds banks that it cannot overflow;" here to a tumultuous and giddy people—"There is a bound to the raging of the sea." Our Constitution is like our island, which uses and restrains its subject sea; in vain the waves roar. In that Constitution I know, and exultingly I feel, both that I am free and that I am not free dangerously to myself or to others. I know that no power on earth, acting as I ought to do, can touch my life, my liberty, or my property. I have that inward and dignified consciousness of my own security and independence, which constitutes, and is the only thing which does constitute, the proud and comfortable sentiment of freedom in the human breast. I know, too, and I bless God for my safe mediocrity; I know that if I possessed all the talents of the gentlemen on the side of the House I sit, and on the other, I cannot, by royal favour, or by popular delusion, or by oligarchical cabal, elevate myself above a certain very limited point, so as to endanger my own fall or the ruin of my country. I know there is an order that keeps things fast in their place; it is made to us, and we are made to it. Why not ask another wife, other children, another body, another mind?

The great object of most of these reformers is to prepare the destruction of the Constitution, by disgracing and discrediting the House of Commons. For they think—prudently, in my opinion—that if they can persuade the nation that the House of Commons is so constituted as not to secure the public liberty; not to have a proper connection with the public interests; so constituted as not, either actually or virtually, to be the representative of the people, it will be easy to prove that a government composed of a monarchy, an oligarchy chosen by the Crown, and such a

House of Commons, whatever good can be in such a system, can by no means be a system of free government.

The Constitution of England is never to have a quietus; it is to be continually vilified, attacked, reproached, resisted; instead of being the hope and sure anchor in all storms, instead of being the means of redress to all grievances, itself is the grand grievance of the nation, our shame instead of our glory. If the only specific plan proposed—individual, personal representation—is directly rejected by the person who is looked on as the great support of this business, then the only way of considering it is as a question of convenience. An honourable gentleman prefers the individual to the present. He therefore himself sees no middle term whatsoever, and therefore prefers of what he sees the individual; this is the only thing distinct and sensible that has been advocated. He has then a scheme, which is the individual representation; he is not at a loss, not inconsistent—which scheme the other right honourable gentleman reprobates. Now, what does this go to, but to lead directly to anarchy? For to discredit the only government which he either possesses or can project, what is this but to destroy all government; and this is anarchy. My right honourable friend, in supporting this motion, disgraces his friends and justifies his enemies, in order to blacken the Constitution of his country, even of that House of Commons which supported him. There is a difference between a moral or political exposure of a public evil, relative to the administration of government, whether in men or systems, and a declaration of defects, real or supposed, in the fundamental Constitution of your country. The first may be cured in the individual by the motives of religion, virtue, honour, fear, shame, or interest. Men may be made to abandon, also, false systems by exposing their absurdity or mischievous tendency to their own better thoughts, or to the contempt or indignation of the public; and after all, if they should exist, and exist uncorrected, they only disgrace individuals as fugitive opinions. But it is quite otherwise with the frame and Constitution of the State; if that is disgraced, patriotism is destroyed in its very source. No man has ever willingly obeyed, much less was desirous of defending with his blood, a mischievous and absurd scheme of government. Our first, our dearest, most comprehensive relation, our country, is gone.

It suggests melancholy reflections, in consequence of the strange course we have long held, that we are now no longer quarrelling about the character, or about the conduct of men, or the tenor of measures; but we are grown out of humour with the English Constitution itself; this is become the object of the animosity of Englishmen. This Constitution in former days used to be the admiration and the envy of the world; it was the pattern for politicians; the theme of the eloquent; the meditation of the philosopher in every part of the world. As to Englishmen, it was their pride, their consolation. By it they lived, for it they were ready to die. Its defects, if it had any, were partly covered by partiality, and partly borne by prudence. Now all its excellencies are forgotten, its faults are now forcibly dragged into day, exaggerated by every artifice of representation. It is despised and rejected of men; and every device and invention of ingenuity, or idleness, set up in opposition or in preference to it. It is to this humour, and it is to the measures growing out of it, that I set myself (I hope not alone) in the most determined opposition. Never before did we at any time in this country meet upon the theory of our frame of government, to sit in judgment on the Constitution of our country, to call it as a delinquent before us, and to accuse it of every defect and every vice; to see whether it, an object of our veneration, even our adoration, did or did not accord with a preconceived scheme in the minds of certain gentlemen. Cast your eyes on the journals of Parliament. It is for fear of losing the inestimable treasure we have, that I do not venture to game it out of my hands for the vain hope of improving it. I look with filial reverence on the Constitution of my country, and never will cut it in pieces, and put it into the kettle of any magician, in order to boil it, with the puddle of their compounds, into youth and vigour. On the contrary, I will drive away such pretenders; I will nurse its venerable age, and with lenient arts extend a parent's breath.

---